"Landmines are everywhere as we walk in our sexually charged culture. Many are directly connected to pornography and its consequences—mental slavery, marriage breakups, sexual infidelity and deep shame. *Every Man a Pure Warrior* maps a way out, but it is not an easy road. Yet the steps are simple and lead to a new and profound freedom."

Jerry White, Ph.D., Retired Major General, USAF, International President Emeritus, The Navigators

"Bob Reehm has made an incredible contribution to the kingdom of God with *Every Man a Pure Warrior*. Addressing purity with men is not a quick fix. Bob guides men into lives of purity based on his depth of walking with Christ, his own battle for purity, and decades of coming alongside men in their purity journeys."

Scott Frickenstein, Ph.D., Col (USAF, ret); Founder and Coach, Leading by Design

"*Every Man a Pure Warrior* takes men deep into God's Word and His plan for purity. Bob's transparency draws you in, realizing you are not alone in this struggle. These principles when learned and put into practice, enable men to turn from lust and pornography. It is wonderful to be freed from impure thinking, to dispel the darkness and experience God in fresh ways!"

Chad Schreur, Adult Discipleship Director, Hillcrest Church, Grand Rapids, MI

"Bob Reehm's decades of disciple-making experience have identified essential principles which refine character, restore confidence, and release captives of sexual addiction and pornography so that they may be free to re-engage in Kingdom life purpose."

Marvin Campbell, Senior Vice-President, The Navigators

"*Every Man a Pure Warrior* has given me freedom from the prison of porn. This study is such a blessing. Instead of daily bondage and struggle, I now have intimacy with God and my wife."

***Every Man A Pure Warrior* field tester.**

"It's been 107 days since the last time I fell off the wagon of purity and a lot has to do with *Every Man a Pure Warrior*."

***Every Man A Pure Warrior* field tester**

"God is working. Through *Every Man a Pure Warrior*, He is reaching the deep parts of my heart with his great love, grace and wisdom. As a leader, it is such a gift to come alongside men and help them see more clearly God's plan for sexual purity. Men in our group found allies that supported them, they grew stronger in the Word and found the seven principles in *Every Man a Pure Warrior* that were the keys to sexual freedom."

Leader of *Every Man A Pure Warrior* field test group

Overview of the *Every Man A Warrior* Series

EVERY MAN A WARRIOR is a discipleship Bible study series for men comprised of four books. Here is how the course is put together:

Book 1 *Walking with God*
The first nine lessons of EVERY MAN A WARRIOR develop the essential skills of discipleship. These skills are: Having a Quiet Time, Meditating on Scripture, Prayer, and Application of the Word. These skills are then applied to the topics in the next two books. It is important that all men go through Book 1 before starting Books 2 and 3. Book 1 includes the EVERY MAN A WARRIOR verse pack and course verses for Books 1-3.

Book 2 *Marriage and Raising Children*
These eight lessons give practical help and a biblical outlook on both Marriage and Raising Children. It comes with a special emphasis on raising teenagers. These lessons have profoundly impacted the lives of men wanting to become better husbands and fathers.

Book 3 *Money, Sex, Work, Hard Times, Making Your Life Count*
Book 3 has ten lessons that bring scriptural application to the issues of Money, Sex and Moral Purity, Work, Going through Hard Times, and How to Make Your Life Count. After family, these are the issues that most consume a man's life and where he needs to succeed.

Single men may choose to use only Books 1 and 3.

Book 4 *Every Man A Pure Warrior*
For men to succeed in life, they must win the battle against pornography and sexual sin. This book presents seven keys or principles that men must master to escape from the prison of porn. These keys form the acronym: WWW A MAP. Worship, Spiritual Warfare, Wounds, Amputate, Memorize Scripture, Allies, and Preach the Gospel to yourself daily. Mastering these seventeen lessons is essential to help men get and stay free from pornography.

Every Man a Warrior

HELPING MEN SUCCEED IN LIFE

Book 4

Every Man A Pure Warrior

BY BOB REEHM

Every Man A Warrior materials are sold exclusively at
www.EveryManAWarrior.com

Every Man A Warrior, Book 4: *Every Man A Pure Warrior*

©2014 Every Man A Warrior, Inc.

All rights reserved. No part of this publication may be reproduced in any form without written permission from , Inc., PO Box 8700, Cary NC. 27512.

ISBN: 978-0-578-68616-5

Some of the anecdotal illustrations in this book are true to life and are included with permission of the persons involved. All other illustrations are composites of real situations, and any resemblance to people living or dead is coincidental.

Unless otherwise identified, all Scripture quotations in this publication are taken from the Holy Bible, New International Version® (NIV®). Copyright © 1973, 1978, 1984 Biblica. Used by permission of Zondervan. All rights reserved. Other versions used include: Revised Standard Version of the Bible (RSV), copyright 1946, 1952, 1971, by the Division of Christian Education of the National Council of the Churches of Christ in the USA, used by permission, all rights reserved; the New American Standard Bible® (NASB), Copyright © 1960, 1962, 1963, 1968, 1971, 1972, 1973, 1975, 1977, 1995 by The Lockman Foundation. Used by permission.

Printed in the United States of America.

4 5 6 7 8 9 10 / 17 16 15 14 13 12

You may download and reproduce any of the resources from the website EveryManAWarrior.com. These have been provided by the author for your benefit.

How to Use This Study

Every Man A Pure Warrior is designed for both married and single men. The assumption is that men will have completed at least Books 1 and 3 of the Every Man A Warrior series. Married men should have also completed Book 2 of EMAW.

To do Book 4 effectively, you will need to be men who are already proficient in walking with God, having consistent Quiet Times, and dedicated to prayer and memorizing Scriptures. If a man has not learned these basics skills taught in the first three books of the Every Man A Warrior series, it is NOT recommended to start *Every Man A Pure Warrior*.

Completing EMAW Books 1-3 with some other men develops spiritual disciplines necessary to go to the deeper levels required in Book 4. During the first three books you will also have learned to trust men with the issues of the heart in the safe environment of a confidential small group under the guidance of a Godly leader. Once these skills are mastered, then start Book 4 and you will have the greatest possibility to succeed in breaking a porn or other addiction.

Once this study begins, it is NOT recommended that new-comers join the study. Each lesson of *Every Man A Pure Warrior* builds on the previous lesson. The trust level and the deep sharing of struggles in the group can only be maintained by the consistent attendance of those committed to complete the group.

In a Small Group

Using *Every Man A Pure Warrior* in a small group of three to six men is optimal. These groups normally meet in the evening. Some groups have met successfully early on Saturday mornings or during the week before work. A time slot of ninety minutes is needed for groups.

One-on-One

Many men have used this as a one-on-one time of discipleship training. For some men, the shame of sexual sin is too great to share in a group.

A Men's Sunday School Class

Every Man A Pure Warrior is NOT recommended for a church Sunday school class, because of the commitment and vulnerability required.

How Every Man A Pure Warrior Came About

I met Lonnie Berger and read through the first three books of Every Man A Warrior. As a fellow Navigator Staff, we both share the passion and calling for making disciples. I felt that more emphasis was needed to help men overcome the plague of pornography. Most of the men that I had the privilege of discipling over my 40 years of ministry were struggling with pornography. Lonnie asked me if I would write Book 4, *Every Man A Pure Warrior*. Hundreds of men have field tested this material. All the stories found in *Every Man A Pure Warrior* are true. The names and the details have been changed to protect confidentiality and privacy.

Note to Leaders

Be sure to follow the Leaders Guide in leading each lesson. It is important to follow the Leader's Guide even if you have led other Bible studies. It has come from two years of field-testing and is designed to help your group succeed. For example, some men find the disciplines of Quiet Times and Scripture memory hard to do and want to skip those parts of the course. Following the Leader's Guide will ensure that these items are not left out and make the Leader's Guide the course disciplinarian, not you! Not all groups make it and it is normal to have some men drop from the course. Using the Leader's Guide gives you the greatest potential to have a successful group.

More than any other study, it is vital that you as the Leader set the proper tone for the men in your study. If you are open, vulnerable and share the failures of your life, you will set an atmosphere of trust for the group. Give the men in your study the "gift of going second". You, the leader, must model repentant humility and leading first to reveal the broken parts of your life. The most successful groups in the field testing were the ones who had leaders who set the pace in vulnerability, and humility.

CONTENTS
BOOK 4

FOREWORD — 1

INTRODUCTION:
Enslaved by Pornography — 3

LESSON 1:
Unlocking the Prison Doors of Pornography — 7

LESSON 2:
Battle Strategy Checklist — 17

LESSON 3:
Allies: Battle Buddies — 29

LESSON 4:
Scripture Memory: Key to Transformation — 43

LESSON 5:
Aggressive Worship Skill 1: Memorize Psalm 103:8-12 — 53

LESSON 6: Aggressive Worship Skill 2: Singing Psalms, Hymns and Spiritual Songs — 63

LESSON 7:
Aggressive Worship Skill 3: Daily Offering and Armoring Our Bodies for Warfare — 73

LESSON 8:
Spiritual Warfare 1: Was I Under Demonic Attack? — 83

LESSON 9:
Spiritual Warfare 2: The Jesus Warfare Model — 99

LESSON 10:
Spiritual Warfare 3: Steps to Resist Demonic Oppression — 111

LESSON 11:
Wounds 1: "Porn Is Meeting a Need in Your Life" — 123

LESSON 12:
Wounds 2: Connecting Your Heart to God — 133

LESSON 13:
 WOUNDS 3: FORGIVENESS: REMOVING THE THORN OF WOUNDEDNESS ... **145**

LESSON 14:
 AMPUTATION AND BLOCKADE ... **157**

LESSON 15:
 PREACH THE GOSPEL TO YOURSELF DAILY ... **167**

LESSON 16:
 RADICAL TRANSFORMATION ... **179**

LESSON 17:
 HOPE: REVIEW AND APPLY ... **193**

APPENDIX

NOTE TO LEADERS	**206**
BIBLICAL FOUNDATIONS FOR SPIRITUAL WARFARE PRAYER	**210**
THE EVERY MAN A WARRIOR ICON	**214**
EMOTIONAL PAIN WORDS	**215**
QUIET TIME JOURNAL	**216**
COMPLETION RECORD	**226**
PURITY PACK NIV VERSES	**229**
MAKING A DIFFERENCE	**231**
ABOUT THE AUTHOR	**232**

Foreword

Men,

You are about to engage in what may in fact be the biggest battle of your life!

I don't say this lightly. The Enemy has brought great evil on the earth. Pornography and lust are satanic perversions of the love God intended between a man and his wife. Pornography constitutes a spiritual pandemic, demonically designed to destroy men's lives.

Christian men have also been captured by this evil. God designed sexual attraction between men and women. And in the context of marriage, it is beautiful, precious, holy and good. The Devil has corrupted this attraction to enslave men to lust.

Not every man going through Book 4 of the Every Man A Warrior series is enslaved to porn. But the principles you learn in this book can set you free from other compulsions as well—sins below the surface such as anger, fear, rage and sexual confusion, along with feelings of worthlessness, shame, rejection and unforgiveness.

In Luke 4, after going through his own battle with Satan in the wilderness, Jesus announced the purpose of his ministry: "to bind up the brokenhearted and to set captives free." *Every Man A Pure Warrior* has the same objective.

Whatever sin has imprisoned you, *Every Man A Pure Warrior* can help and will give you a step-by-step process to open the prison doors and walk through to freedom. Plus, the process learned in this book will help you disciple other men who are struggling with porn or similar addictions.

But the Enemy does not give up his captives without a fight. That's why I believe you are about to enter into a great battle. During our field test, some men dropped out of the course. So, men, resolve that you will fight hard, harder than ever before, to be set free. Commit yourself to the process and the whole course. You will have allies. In Week 2, you will pair up with a fellow Warrior participant to become safe, confidential partners who can call each other for support when temptation looms.

In 2018, Bob Reehm and I sat down together to seek the Lord and pray for His guidance on this project. We sensed that the Lord wanted to give Bob the keys to unlock the multiple layers of prison doors that must be opened if a man is to break out of an addiction. Bob calls the resulting process WWW A MAP, and no other resource has all seven steps. You will get acquainted with WWW A MAP in the first lesson.

Be courageous, men. Christ died for you to be free.

In the battle with you,
Lonnie Berger
Author and President of Every Man A Warrior

INTRODUCTION: ENSLAVED BY PORNOGRAPHY

I believe pornography is the greatest cancer in the Church today.
—Charles Swindoll

Before the Every Man A Warrior series was published, I had the privilege of reading a rough draft. I called Lonnie Berger and told him that everything in books 1-3 was gold. Men needed to read and study the material. But I also challenged him. Almost every man whom I had been meeting with for discipleship was enslaved to pornography. I told Lonnie, "You have thirty-seven lessons for men but only one lesson on moral purity. I think this needs to be bulked up." He agreed and invited me to write Book 4 of the series. This has been a five-year writing project, unofficially field-tested by numerous groups of men who have all given excellent feedback and suggestions for improvement. This study is a culmination of a lifelong pursuit of holiness. As you read in the following lessons, a lot of this is autobiographical. All identities in the stories have been changed and sometimes are a combination of several stories.

Anytime statistics are mentioned, they are almost always immediately out of date. This is especially true in the area of pornography. Below are recent statistics for pornography. In several years, based on current trends, unless God intervenes with a worldwide revival, they will only be worse.

10 Ugly Numbers Describing Pornography Use in 2017

We all know that the world has become pornified and that the internet has made available to all of us an entire universe of pornographic content. Yet many of the statistics we rely on and commonly quote have become outdated. As technology changes and as new generations grow up, the pornographic landscape inevitably changes. I went looking for updated numbers and want to present some of them to you today. All of these are based on credible studies carried out in 2016 or 2017.

In 2016, people watched 4.6 billion hours of pornography on just one website (the biggest porn site in the world). That's 524,000 years of porn or, if you will, around 17,000 complete lifetimes. In that same time, people watched 92 billion videos (or an average of 12.5 for every person on earth). Significance: So many people are using so much porn today that it is impossible to tabulate. But understanding how much is consumed at just one site can at least help us see that this problem is nothing less than an epidemic.

At age **eleven**, the average child has already been exposed to explicit pornographic content through the internet. Twenty-two percent of the vast quantities of porn consumed by people aged under eighteen is consumed by those aged less than ten.

Seventy percent of young adults define porn by its function, not its form.

Fifty-seven percent of young adults admit to seeking out porn at least once per month.

Ninety-six percent of young adults are either encouraging, accepting, or neutral in their view toward pornography. That leaves only a tiny minority who consider it a negative thing. Only one in twenty young adults say their friends consider porn a bad thing.

Sixty-one percent of pornography is watched on a mobile phone. In the United States that is as high as 70 percent.

Today, **thirty-three percent** of women aged twenty-five and under go searching for porn at least once per month.

Sixty-two percent of teens and young adults have received a sexually explicit image. Meanwhile, 41 percent have sent one, usually to their boyfriend or girlfriend.

Thirty-six percent of young adults watch pornography to get tips or ideas that they can apply to their own sexual relationships. Eighty percent of porn users feel no sense of guilt when using porn.

Conclusion

These numbers prove statistically what we already know anecdotally—that pornography is a significant issue afflicting our society and our church. As Christians, we can and must be prepared to help those who are struggling with it and to assure them that they can be forgiven and freed. As parents, we can and must take action to protect and equip our children so we can help them overcome and avoid it.[1]

Finally, one more ugly number was reported on June 6, 2019, by Kimberly Leonard, of the Washington Examiner: more than 1 million new STD infections daily.

> **PURPOSE STATEMENT** This study is designed to help anyone understand and overcome enslavement to pornography. It lays a groundwork that covers the spiritual idolatry of porn, the psychological needs that porn fraudulently promises to meet, the discipleship response required of a follower of Jesus, the spiritual warfare aspect of porn, and how to help another person who has been defiled by porn.

There are seven keys, or principles, that must be both understood and practiced. These seven keys form the acronym **WWW A MAP**. They stand for:

Worship
Warfare Praying
Wounds and Triggers
Amputate
Memorize Scripture
Allies
Preach the Gospel to Yourself Daily

---

[1] Tim Challies, from www.challies.com/articles/10-ugly-and-updated-numbers-about-pornography-use/. Used with permission.

One of your assignments will be to memorize this list of principles. To fulfill the requirements of this study, you will need to practice it a hundred times so that you both know and understand it backward and forward. You will be asked to practice WWW A MAP every day during the course and to record each week the number of times you practiced these principles.

LESSON 1
Unlocking the Prison Doors of Pornography

- ✓ Leaders, before leading this study, please go to the Appendix and read "Note to Leaders."

- ✓ Open the session with prayer.

- ✓ Ask the men to review their favorite EMAW verses.

- ✓ Begin by reading the Introduction, out loud, and discussing it paragraph by paragraph.

- ✓ Discuss each of the questions in this lesson.

- ✓ Lookup and read each verse together. Try to get everyone to participate.

- ✓ Depending on time, have as many men as possible share their *Ask Questions*, meditations, and rewrites of 1 Corinthians 10:13.

- ✓ Read the *Points to Remember* and the *Assignment*.

- ✓ End this session by closing with prayer, using the *WAR* method.

Unlocking the Prison Doors of Porn

Several years ago I was asked to do a daylong seminar on sexual purity at Soledad State Prison in California. It is a maximum-security prison housing more than five thousand prisoners. A secure prison, it has cells, fences, walled perimeters, electronic security, and armed guards both within and outside the walls.

After background checks were completed, the day came for the seminar. An armed guard led me through the first outer secured perimeter, then through another electronically controlled, barred gate. Then I was led through a maze and another locked jail door. My armed escort then led me through two more gates. Each time, the guard had to signal to another guard to open the gate to let us through. Finally, after going through six barred gates, there was one more guarded entry door to get into the room where the seminar was to take place.

My experience at the prison is a picture of the battle that all of us are in: to get and stay pure. If a prisoner tried to escape, it would be a daunting task. If he were to escape the first level of restraint, he would then have to get through the next level of enslavement. Then he would have to figure out how to get out of the ensuing four levels of prison bars and surveillance before he could finally get through the last barrier to obtain freedom from captivity. It was a prison within a prison times seven, just like the prison of pornography.

For thirty years I was enslaved by porn. When I was ten years old, I naively entered the prison of porn. I didn't know Christ. I simply indulged my passions—lusting, consuming porn, and masturbating frequently. When I was seventeen, I became a believer and for a few weeks felt forgiven. But I was still enslaved and quickly reverted to the lust-porn-masturbation cycle. I even memorized a verse, 1 Corinthians 10:13: *"No temptation has overtaken you except what is common to mankind. And God is faithful; he will not let you be tempted beyond what you can bear. But when you are tempted, he will also provide a way out so that you can endure it."*

A year later I went to college and joined a fellowship group. The men shared hundreds of prayer requests over the next three years, but not one man shared anything related to sexual struggles or purity or holiness. I concluded that I was the only person who struggled with lust. I also concluded that 1 Corinthians 10:13 was not true. My continual temptations were not "common to mankind." I felt that I was an exception, that my sex drive was unusually virile, that my sins were too strong, and that God had not provided a way of escape.

One day one of my friends told me that God was leading him to seek me out and confess some sin to me. I had no idea what he was going to say. He was afraid to share his hidden, secret life with me. He made me promise not to tell anyone. He finally mustered up enough courage to say, "I look at pornography and masturbate almost every day."

I couldn't believe it. I asked him, "Are you lying to me?" He said, "No." An awkward silence followed. As I stared at him, I felt a deep sense of joy welling up in me, and I hugged him and said, "Me too." I was not alone!

I approached five of my closest buddies separately, and I privately said to each one, "I am going to tell you something and then ask you something. Will you promise to be honest with me?" Each man assured me that he would. I told each one a brief history of my involvement with lust, porn, and masturbation and then asked, "I've been around you now for several years, and not once have I heard you mention that this might be a struggle for you. Do you battle these things too?" Each man bowed his head and mumbled, "Me too." I learned that sexual sins are addictive and common to every man.

As a Christian, I had been in a solitary confinement cell of shame, silence, and guilt. I had felt alone and isolated and had no idea that there was a whole prison filled with people just like me. I had tried and failed so many times that I had no hope that I could ever get free. I read books, sought counsel, cried out to God, fasted, and read more books. I tried everything I could but still found myself enslaved to lust, porn, and masturbation. It wasn't until my friend received the God-given courage to come and speak to me that I found out that I was not alone. This was the start of a decades-long battle as I struggled to escape from the prison of porn.

In 2005, I started experiencing freedom. God graciously heard my cry, and He answered my prayers. Our loving heavenly Father began showing me step by step how to unlock the prison doors of porn so I could be set free.

THIS STUDY WILL SHOW YOU SEVEN PRIMARY KEYS OR PRINCIPLES THAT GOD REVEALED TO ME, FREEING ME FROM THE PRISON OF PORN. THESE PRINCIPLES ARE NOT NEGOTIABLE. THEY MUST BE UNDERSTOOD, TRUSTED IN, AND APPLIED DAILY FOR YOU TO START TO SEE FREEDOM. JUST LIKE AN ANCIENT LOCK THESE ARE KEYS TO FREEDOM. THESE PRINCIPLES FORM THE ACRONYM: **WWW A MAP.**

Here is an overview of the study and a summary of these seven keys:

1. Worship: We must become great worshipers of Jesus. We must learn how to exchange our worship of porn and adoration of the human body for continuous worship and praise of our Creator God.

2. Warfare Praying: We must learn how to overcome the Evil One and learn the principles of spiritual warfare praying. This includes learning about Satan, his tactics, and how to use the weapons that the Lord has given to us.

3. Wounds and Triggers: We must understand our wounds and what triggers us to self-medicate. With God's help, we must learn how to receive healing for our woundedness. Our culture offers a multitude of Band-Aids to try to ease our pain: food, gambling, drugs, etc. This study will focus on porn, lust, and masturbation as Band-Aids, but the seven principles, if applied, will work for any sin that masters us.

> **As a Christian, I had been in a solitary confinement cell of shame, silence, and guilt. I had felt alone and isolated and had no idea that there was a whole prison filled with people just like me.**

4. Amputate and Block: We must take all necessary steps to remove porn and block all access to pornography in our lives. These steps require lifestyle changes and are referred to as radical amputation.

5. Memorize Verses: We are commanded to take every thought captive to the obedience of Christ. The only way to do this is to intentionally memorize and continually meditate on these memorized Scriptures.

6. Allies: We cannot do this alone. We need brothers around us to encourage us, challenge us, and pick us up if and when we fall. We must learn both how to be allies to others and how to encourage and be encouraged in the mutual battle.

7. Preach the Gospel to Yourself Daily: The only hope to escape enslavement is through the radical life and teachings of Jesus our Savior. We must understand our position and authority in Christ and preach the gospel to ourselves every day.

> *Porn is a form of worship. We worshiped our way into addiction; we must worship our way out. We must become great worshipers of Jesus.*

This book, *Every Man A Pure Warrior*, may be the most challenging Bible study you will ever attempt to complete. It is essential that you have completed at least the first two books of the Every Man A Warrior series, and we highly recommend that you have finished all three.

Every Man A Pure Warrior builds on the skills learned in EMAW. If the habits of Quiet Time, Scripture memory, prayer, meditation, and worship have not yet become consistent in your life, it is likely that you will struggle in freeing yourself from a habit of consuming porn.

The skills of Quiet Time, Scripture memory, prayer, meditation, and worship are your weapons of war. These disciplines allow us to learn about and receive the grace and spiritual power from the Lord Jesus that we will need to fight and win this battle. This is why we recommend that you have at least two books of the EMAW series under your belt before you begin this course.

Some men will start the study but, fall out before completion. It will take courage and hard work to win this battle. But the reward at the end will be freedom from enslavement to sin, a transformed life, and the ability to help set other men free from their prison of porn (Romans 12:2).

We will need to create a safe environment to share our struggles. It takes courage to talk about porn, lust, and masturbation. Real men of God have this courage (Philippians 1:19-21). A safe environment with other like-minded men greatly enhances our ability to win our battle with porn and other addictions.

Please look over the following commitment pledge. Pray through it. If you sense that the Holy Spirit is leading you to be a part of this study with these men at this time in your life, then please sign it.

✓ **Leaders**: Please make sure that each man signs this pledge of commitment before continuing.

MY COMMITMENT

Because of the nature of this study, it is important to renew your commitment to certain vital concepts and principles. Please look at the following commitment pledge, then sign at the bottom.

One of the most potentially embarrassing things to know about someone is his struggle in the area of sexual or other enslaving sins. There is great risk in sharing this part of our lives and hearts. Proverbs 11:13 says, "A gossip betrays a confidence, but a trustworthy person keeps a secret."

MY COMMITMENT

I promise to keep secrets that are divulged in this group. What is shared in the group will remain in the group. I will not disclose another man's secrets or confessions. If married, I will not share things heard with my wife.

I will to the best of my abilities complete the lessons and come each week ready to share what the Holy Spirit has taught me.

I will not act shocked or disgusted with what another person shares with me or within the group. Sin, like gangrene, is progressive and deadly (James 1:12-15). What starts as fantasy may end up something that society considers deplorable. One of the fundamental principles in the Scriptures to help us walk in purity is a band of brothers who will walk alongside us, hearing our confessions and failures (James 5:16) and offering hope and help along our journey (Hebrews 3:13). I endeavor to be that kind of man with the others in my group.

Sign your name: _____

✓ How important is it to you that we each sign this commitment to confidentiality?

Let's be clear. This will be war. Confronting the use of porn in your own life or others' lives will cause the Enemy to respond. Porn has created a spiritual stronghold, and the demons of porn will fight to remain in control. This battle will not be won without courage, faith, a safe environment, and a deep relationship with God. For most men, it is the biggest spiritual battle they will ever face.

✓ Do you believe the above paragraph to be true? Why or why not?

✓ Why is it that Christian men don't talk about porn, lust, or masturbation? Is this silence helpful or not?

✓ Briefly share with your group your porn and lust history. Share a sanitized version—no pornographic details. Each man should share for a maximum of three to five minutes.

✓ What do you hope to gain from this study? Be prepared to share with the group.

✓ **Leaders**: Please record what each man hopes to gain from this study. Keep these answers confidential. Review their respective own reasons with any men in your group who are tempted to drop out of the study or who have become discouraged.

ASSIGNMENT 1: Memorize and be able to recite the first card in order. WWW A MAP:

Worship
Warfare Praying
Wounds and Triggers
Amputate
Memorize Scripture
Allies
Preach the Gospel to Yourself Daily

ASSIGNMENT 2: Memorize 1 Corinthians 10:13.

No temptation has overtaken you except what is common to mankind. And God is faithful; he will not let you be tempted beyond what you can bear. But when you are tempted, he will also provide a way out so that you can endure it.
—1 Corinthians 10:13

✓ Meditate on 1 Corinthians 10:13, using the *Ask Questions* method. Jot down two or three observations.

Ask Questions

Is there:

A command to obey

A promise to claim

A sin to avoid

An application to make

Something new about God

Ask: Who, What, When, Where, Why

Emphasize:
Different words

Rewrite
In your own words

✓ Rewrite 1 Corinthians 10:13 in your own words. Be prepared to share this with the group.

✓ How does 1 Corinthians 10:13 affect your attitude and your relationships with others in your group?

Points to Remember

1. Sexual sins are enslaving and common to every person.

2. It takes courage to talk about porn, lust, and masturbation. Real men of God have this courage.

3. A safe environment with other like-minded men will greatly enhance the ability of men to win the battle with porn.

✓ To summarize this lesson, write out the most important things you learned.

Assignment for Next Week

1. Have your Quiet Times this week: Psalm 62:8, Psalm 46, Psalm 23, and Psalm 27. Focus on the idea of God as our refuge.

2. Try to record five to seven Quiet Times this week. It is okay to use one of your Quiet Times to complete the lesson and one Quiet Time to review verses and work on your current memory verse.

3. Be prepared to share all your EMAW Book 1 verses for next week.

4. Practice the WAR (Worship, Admit, Request) method of prayer in your Quiet Times this week. Begin praying for the men in your group to have consistent and quality times with the Lord. Pray against the Enemy's attacking the Quiet Times of the men in the group.

5. Memorize the first card in your *Every Man A Pure Warrior* verse pack with the acronym WWW A MAP. When you can quote in order, these the seven steps, then place the memory card with 1 Corinthians 10:13 in the front window of your verse pack and memorize it also.

6. Study and complete lesson 2 before next week's group meeting.

A Very Important Concluding Note

At this stage in the study, if lust, pornography, and masturbation are an ongoing and previously undisclosed struggle for you, I am asking you to not tell your wife. As you grow and learn the steps of freedom, at some point in the future it may be appropriate and wise to tell her. This will be discussed further in lesson 16.

For some men, if their wife has been abused, raped, or struggles with depression, it may never be wise to burden her with their own sin. Either way, we trust the Holy Spirit to lead and guide us when or if it is right to tell her.

LESSON 2
BATTLE STRATEGY CHECKLIST

✓ Have the men break into pairs and recite the first two memory cards to each other (WWW A MAP and 1 Corinthians 10:13). Also, have them recite all their EMAW Book 1 verses. Have one man hold the cards and say the reference while the other quotes the verse and says the reference at the end of the verse. Then have them switch roles.

✓ Sign off on anything finished on the *Completion Records*.

✓ Open the session with prayer.

✓ Ask each of the men if he has signed the My Commitment pledge on page 12. If not have them sign it now.

✓ Go around the room, asking each man to share one Quiet Time.

✓ Begin reading the lesson paragraph by paragraph.

✓ Discuss each of the questions.

✓ Lookup and read each verse together. Try to get everyone to participate.

✓ Depending on time, have as many men as possible share their *Ask Questions*, meditations and their rewrites of Ephesians 5:3.

✓ Read the *Points to Remember* and the *Assignment*.

This lesson is a summary of this entire study. These seven fundamental truths, or skills, need to be mastered and practiced every day. Thinks of these as separate keys unlocking seven different levels of prisons. Each succeeding lesson will focus on the one aspect of the checklist, giving background, verses, and correlating stories.

Battle Strategy Checklist

I served in the U.S. Navy as a nuclear engineer on nuclear-powered ships. After a year and a half of intensive training, I was ready to "assume the watch" and reported to the USS Enterprise as a reactor officer. One of my jobs was to oversee the start-up of nuclear reactors. We began with a multiple-page document explaining how to safely start up a nuclear reactor. Every valve and every switch in the engineering and reactor rooms had to be checked to ensure absolute safety and control of the reactor. Failure to completely follow the checklist could lead to catastrophic failure for the reactor, the crew, the ship, and even the defense of the nation.

It was a tedious process. Because of the high potential for human error, no one was allowed to complete the checklist by himself. Every valve and switch position had to be verified and reported on by two people. Think of that: check and recheck, every valve and every switch double-checked. The stakes were that high.

Over the years God has taught me seven key principles in the battle to get and stay morally pure. I practice these every day. They are my battle strategy checklist. These concepts or principles are easy to understand but take time to learn and put into practice.

> A summary of each fundamental principle is briefly discussed in this lesson. The intent is for you to become immediately exposed to these principles and to start developing the skill set and to practice them. One of the assignments for every lesson going forward in this course is for you to mentally, spiritually, and personally go through each skill and each principle every day until this course is complete. As you review these skills every day for almost one hundred days, hopefully, they'll become second nature to you, and you'll know how to fight and win the battle for sexual freedom and how to teach and help other men to get and stay pure.

These seven principles form the acronym WWW A MAP. This curriculum focuses on giving you a map and the seven keys to escape from the prison of porn or any enslaving, compulsive sin.

Worship

Warfare Praying

Wounds and Triggers

Amputation

Memorize Scripture

Allies

Preach the Gospel to Yourself Daily

Principle 1: Aggressive Worship

We worship our way into an addiction; we worship our way out of an addiction.

There are three skills of worship that need to be mastered. These skills are:
1. Quoting and worshiping through portions of Psalm 103 or other psalms of worship and praise.
2. Singing from the heart a God-centered hymn, psalm, or spiritual song.
3. Learning how to put on daily our spiritual armor and the offering of our body and body parts to God as a sacrifice of worship.

For any skill to be active and useful in our lives, we must practice it over and over again until there are both muscle memory and mental habits are formed. When the flesh demands to be satisfied, we need to train ourselves to immediately run to worship God aggressively.

Aggressive Worship—Skill 1:
Worship God by Quoting Psalm 103:8-12, Colossians 1:15-20, or Philippians 2:5-11.

✓ **Leaders**: Have each man open his Bible and read Psalm 103:8-12. Have each man, in turn, share his prayer. For example, Psalm 103:8 says, "The Lord is compassionate and gracious, slow to anger, abounding in love." Pray something like, **"Father, I bless You and worship You with all of my soul. I praise You that You are loving to me and that You are slow to anger."** (The memory assignment for Lesson 5 is to memorize Psalm 103:8-12.)

Aggressive Worship—Skill 2:
Sing Out Loud or Quote the Words of Your Favorite Hymn, Psalm, or Spiritual Song

Music is a direct conduit into our souls, either for good or for ill. We hear a song sung to a catchy tune, and it does not take many repetitions before we have memorized it. Scripture teaches us in Ephesians 5:19 to address "one another in psalms and hymns and spiritual songs, singing and making melody" (ESV).

Aggressive Worship—Skill 3:
Put on the Armor of God

We are commanded by the Lord both to put on the armor of God to prepare for the spiritual war that we are daily engaged in; and to offer our bodies as living sacrifices, which is our spiritual act of worship.

✓ **Leaders**: Have someone lookup and read Ephesians 6:11 and Romans 12:1.

Principle 2: Warfare Praying

Jesus modeled Warfare Praying for us. In the Lord's Prayer, He specifically addresses temptations and Satan. When you are tempted and under attack, train yourself to practice praying the Lord's Prayer. Personalize it for your situation. Instead of simply saying the words in vain repetition, name your temptation. For example, **"Lead me not into the temptation of lust. Deliver me from the tempter. Deliver me from the deceiver and all his deceptions. Deliver me from the slanderer that is accusing me and calling me names."**

James 4:7 says that if we resist the Devil, he will flee from us. The Lord's Prayer is one example of Warfare Praying. Another example of effective Warfare Praying is found in the Appendix on page 211.

✓ **Leaders**: Have the men in your group pray the following prayer. Pray it in unison, by faith, in the name of Jesus and under the blood of Jesus. Tell the men that every time they are tempted they should pray the Lord's Prayer.

"Our Father in heaven, hallowed be your name, your kingdom come, your will be done, on earth as it is in heaven. Give us today our daily bread, and forgive us our debts, as we also have forgiven our debtors. And lead us not into temptation, but deliver us from the evil one, for yours is the kingdom and the power and the glory forever. Amen." —Matthew 6:9-13 NIV

Principle 3: Wounds and Triggers

Almost all lust, porn, and masturbation (or other things that we become addicted or enslaved to such as video games, eating disorders, gambling and drugs, including recreational marijuana, and nicotine) are forms of self-medication. We feel hurt or get triggered by a past wound, and we want to deaden the pain. The world, Satan, and our flesh find ways to numb or deaden the pain through pleasure or escape. I used to think that consuming porn was helping me escape the chaos of a broken home and an absentee father. It offered refuge and pleasure for a while, but it enslaved me in the process. Ultimately, all hurts and wounds will lead to the need to forgive those who have wounded us. We will need to choose to forgive as the Lord chose to forgive us.

Principle 4: Radical Amputation

Jesus said, *"If your right eye causes you to stumble, gouge it out and throw it away... And if your right hand causes you to stumble, cut it off and throw it away."* —Matthew 5:29-30

Figuratively, we do the same thing when we block all access to pornography. *We need to make a "radical amputation" of all stashes of pornography and all access to porn.* Pornography always has a platform or a delivery system to penetrate through our eyes or ears to get into our minds. The primary method today is through smartphones, laptop computers, tablets, and movies. We need to be ruthless in guarding our ways from temptation.

Getting rid of our collections of porn or our access to porn or harmful relationships may be the hardest thing this course requires. It may be that you are not yet ready to make such a decision. If this is the case, please do not lie to your brothers and say that you've gotten rid of your porn when you know you haven't. If you are not yet ready to rid yourself of porn and access to porn, begin now, asking God for more grace and more power to rid yourself of porn or to break off any relationships that cause you to stumble sexually.

> ✓ **Leaders**: Have each man tell the group either what he has done to limit or destroy his access to porn or what he needs to do to shut the door to ongoing exposure to porn.

Principle 5: Memorize Massive Amounts of Scripture

Sexual sin is unlike any other sin that we commit. It stains our whole inner man and defiles our souls. Once seen, a sexual image can never be unseen. It's burned into our minds. Our brains register it, and it can never be forgotten. It can, however, through the cleansing power of the eternal Word of God be washed and cleansed and our brains transformed. Romans 12:2 says *"Be transformed by the renewing of your mind."* Scripture memory is not optional in this struggle.

> ✓ At the peak of your involvement in sexual sin, when you were looking for and consuming pornography, how much time were you spending on lust? Are you willing to spend at least half of that time memorizing and reviewing Scripture? Why or why not?

The appendix of this book has a list of suggested Bible verses and passages to memorize. These verses all apply to the areas of sexual purity, holiness, and discipleship. Once you've completed this course, memorizing these verses will provide you with additional support for your continued spiritual growth.

Principle 6: Allies

Most men don't have another man or a group of men who truly know their history of sin, vulnerabilities, and habits. Ecclesiastes 4:9-12 says, "Two are better than one, because they have a good return for their labor: If either of them falls down, one can help the other up. But pity anyone who falls and has no one to help them up. Also, if two lie down together, they will keep warm. But how can one keep warm alone? Though one may be overpowered, two can defend themselves. A cord of three strands is not quickly broken."

The skill of being a purity ally revolves around the five previously written principles.

✓ Choose from within your *Every Man A Pure Warrior* group, who will be your allies? If you need to talk to someone and your primary ally is not available, who is the second ally that you will call? Who is the third? Be prepared to share with the group.

1. Ally: _____ Phone:_____
2. Ally: _____ Phone:_____
3. Ally: _____ Phone:_____

Principle 7: Preach the Gospel to Yourself Daily

The gospel, the good news of Jesus dying on the cross, means that He paid the ransom price for all our sins, including all our sexual sins. We are no longer under condemnation or the wrath of God. Our true identities have fundamentally changed, and God has chosen us and adopted us as His sons. Our response in prayer to these truths will be: **"I thank You Father, for the truth that there is now no condemnation for those who are in Christ. Jesus, I thank You for dying on the cross for me. I praise You that I am forgiven. You look at me as if I had never sinned, and I am adopted into Your family. You purchased me, and now I am free from sin."**

WWW A MAP: These seven principles must be practiced daily until they become second nature. We need to both know them by heart and understand the biblical foundations for them. These principles have been vital for me in transforming and rebuilding a defiled, polluted mind. They have given me hope and ongoing encouragement in the battle.

I used to think that victory was not possible. At times, consuming porn, lusting, and masturbating dominated my life so much that I became hopeless and felt powerless to stop my behavior. This enslavement led to depression and thoughts of self-harm. I had no idea of the connections between my father's adultery and the choices I made to self-medicate when I was a young, pre-adolescent male. I had no understanding of spiritual warfare or how I was opening doors to demonic activity. I was untrained in the Scriptures and underestimated the power of Scripture memory. I did not understand the amazing truths of the gospel. It was hit or miss with accountability partners. In short, all seven of these principles needed to be learned, understood, and applied to get and stay morally pure.

Galatians 5:1, 13 says, *"It is for freedom that Christ has set us free. Stand firm, then, and do not let yourselves be burdened again by a yoke of slavery .... You, my brothers and sisters, were called to be free. But do not use your freedom to indulge the flesh; rather, serve one another humbly in love."*

Sadly, many Christian men are not free. Something has them locked in chains. It could be gambling, drugs, alcohol, video games, work, an eating disorder, (being overweight because of eating for comfort or being anorexic because of a fear of getting fat), exercise, or achievement; but the number one issue enslaving our culture is pornography and lust.

> **For any skill to be active and useful in our lives, we must practice it over and over again until both muscle memory and mental habits are formed.**

Please note that these are discipleship principles. In no way am I stating or implying that taking these steps is a way to earn salvation. When Jesus died on the cross, He paid our redemption price in full, adopted us, and made us new creations. By taking these steps, we are not earning sonship or God's favor. But they will help us in our pursuit of growing into the holiness that God has called us to live out daily.

ASSIGNMENT: Memorize Ephesians 5:3.

But among you there must not be even a hint of sexual immorality, or of any kind of impurity, or of greed, because these are improper for God's holy people. —Ephesians 5:3

✓ Meditate on Ephesians 5:3, using the *Ask Questions* method. Jot down two to three thoughts.

✓ Rewrite Ephesians 5:3 in your own words. Be prepared to share this with the group.

> **Ask Questions**
>
> **Is there:**
>
> A command to obey
>
> A promise to claim
>
> A sin to avoid
>
> An application to make
>
> Something new about God
>
> Ask: Who, What, When, Where, Why
>
> **Emphasize:**
> Different words
>
> **Rewrite**
> In your own words

Points to Remember

For any skill to be active and useful in our lives, we must practice it over and over again until both muscle memory and mental habits are formed.

1. We must join the fight in engaging in successful spiritual warfare, learning how to recognize and overcome the Evil One.

2. We must learn our triggers and receive healing from our wounds.

3. We must be ruthless with our choices and practice radical amputation—removing all porn and access to porn from our lives.

4. We must develop a lifelong commitment to memorize Scriptures and meditate on them.

5. We must commit to and develop allies, buddies to aid us in our warfare.

6. We must grow comfortable in the preaching of the gospel to ourselves daily, focusing on the completed work of Christ as given to us in the gospel and reckoning ourselves as dead to sin.

7. We must grow and develop to become great worshipers of God.

✓ To summarize this lesson, write out the most important things you learned.

✓ **Leaders**: As a group read the WWW A MAP Battle Strategy Checklist on page 27. Then ask the men to discuss if this is something they think they could do.

Assignment for Next Week

1. Memorize Ephesians 5:3.

2. Have all your Quiet Times this week and in the next week in the following passages: Ecclesiastes 4:9-10, 2 Timothy 2:20-22, Proverbs 27:17, Galatians 6:1-2, 1 Thessalonians 5:14, and Hebrews 3:13.

3. Try to record five to seven Quiet Times this week in your journal.

4. Complete lesson 3 prior to your next group meeting.

5. Practice the seven critical principles for freedom (WWW A MAP) every day this week, working toward becoming a pure warrior. We will record the number of times you practiced each week.

BATTLE STRATEGY CHECKLIST

Worship

- Start worshiping God by praising Him. Sing your favorite hymn, psalm, or worship song. Offer your body and body parts to God as an act of worship and clothe your body with the armor of God.

Warfare Praying

- First, confess any known sin by praying and say the following spiritual warfare prayer. "Lord Jesus, I ask forgiveness for _____ [name any sin that comes to mind such as looking at porn, masturbation, lust, anger, unforgiveness, greed, or hate]."

- Pray the Lord's Prayer: "Our Father in heaven, hallowed be your name, your kingdom come, your will be done, on earth as it is in heaven. Give us today our daily bread, and forgive us our debts, as we also have forgiven our debtors. And lead us not into temptation, but deliver us from the evil one, for yours is the kingdom and the power and the glory forever. Amen" (Matthew 6:9-13).

- After praying the prayer, personalize it for your temptation. "Lord, please deliver me from the Tempter who is tempting me to _____. Lord, please deliver me from the Accuser who is telling me that my sin is not forgiven." If you are praying with a partner, the partner should say, "I agree in the name of Jesus."

Wounds and Triggers

- Ask the Holy Spirit to show you any wounds that are causing you to act out. Extend forgiveness to anyone who has hurt you. "Lord, I extend forgiveness to_____ for _____."

Amputate

- Separate yourself from any source of porn or lust-inducing environments. If you have just seen a pretty woman who is triggering you, begin to pray for her salvation, that she would find Christ and walk with Him.

Memorize Scripture

- Review your Scripture verses. Begin quoting out loud the verses from Psalm 103, Romans 6, EMAW verses, or any other memorized passages of Scripture.

Allies

- Call a brother for prayer when tempted, confess if you have blown it, and begin to go through these seven principles together.

Preach the Gospel to Yourself Daily

- "I thank You, Father, for the truth that 'there is now no condemnation for those who are in Christ Jesus' (Romans 8:1). I thank You, Jesus, for dying on the cross for me. I praise You that I am forgiven. You look at me as if I had never sinned, and I am adopted into Your family. You purchased me, and now I am free from sin."

WWW A MAP SEVEN KEYS TO FREEDOM

LESSON 3
ALLIES: BATTLE BUDDIES

✓ Have the men break into pairs and recite all their *Every Man A Pure Warrior* verses, beginning with Ephesians 5:3. Have one man hold the card and say the reference while the other quotes the verse and says the reference at the end of the verse. Then have them switch roles.

✓ Sign off on the *completion records* in the back of the book.

✓ Open the session with prayer.

✓ Go around the room, asking each man to share one Quiet Time.

✓ Begin reading the lesson paragraph by paragraph.

✓ Discuss each of the questions on these pages.

✓ Lookup and read each verse together. Try to get everyone to participate.

✓ Have every man read his summary of the need for buddies.

✓ Depending on time, have as many men as possible share their *Ask Questions*, meditations and their rewrites of Ecclesiastes 4:9-10.

✓ Read the *Points to Remember* and the *Assignment*.

✓ Break into pairs and practice WWW A MAP with each other. After one man works through it, have them reverse the roles.

If One of You Blows It: Jon's Story

Jon lived in campus housing with three of his rugby teammates. Each had his own bedroom, but they shared a common area. All four were believers, and all attended the same campus ministry group. But all four struggled with internet porn.

Their campus Bible study leader encouraged them to pray together weekly and to find allies, to help them grow spiritually. But they suffered through agonizing cycles of pornography and confession. And this persisted for eight more weeks.

The following week at the campus fellowship gathering, the topic was spiritual warfare and the power of fasting. At their weekly prayer meeting, Jon challenged his three roommates to change their routines. Jon said, "I feel led to pray and fast about my enslavement to lust, porn, and masturbation. If I stumble this week, I will spend the next twenty-four hours fasting from food. Will any of you join me in this challenge?" Jon went on saying, "If one of you falters, I challenge you too to fast and pray for the next twenty-four hours, and I will fast with you also. In other words, if you fall, I will fast; if I fall, you will fast also. What do you say? Can we all make a pact and agree to this?"

> **Internet porn accountability software is an essential tool to protect you and your family from sinful adult content. There are a number of excellent companies recommended by various Christian organizations: Covenant Eyes, Net Nanny, CYBERsitter, Pure Sight PC, Bsecure Online, True Vine, and Promise Keeper's PKFamily.**

All four stared at each other, letting the challenge seep deeply into their souls. They had all heard the same message, and it had profoundly challenged them all. Tiny (who was not tiny; he was six feet, six inches tall and weighed 280 pounds) said, "I like my food. I don't want to fast ... ever. You are saying that if one of you weaklings blows it, I can't eat?" They all nodded. Tiny hesitated and after a long while said, "Okay, I'll do it. But if one of you blows it, I'm going to smash you." They all felt the impact of those words. They all believed that Tiny would indeed smash them.

The next day, all four met and prayed together before heading off to class. They agreed that they should pray together daily instead of just weekly, and they also agreed to install Covenant Eyes on their computers. Each morning they would pray for each other's purity and that none would fall. They were becoming allies in the battle for holiness and purity.

No one fell that day or the next or the next week. The power of fasting and the camaraderie of the fellowship turned their behavior around. It was six months before one of the four blew it. They kept their agreement to fast, and Tiny showed his buddy some grace instead of smashing him.

> ✓ What impressed you from Jon's story? How important was it that Jon had allies in his fight against porn?

Character Traits of a Good Ally

Accountability is a buzzword used a lot in Christian circles. Unfortunately, it seems to almost always carry an air of fear with it. The normal expectations of accountability partners are that you report after the fact that you've blown it, and an accountability partner might then condemn or shame you in hopes that this will force you to do better next week. When this happens over time, if or when you blow it, you simply stop going to your accountability partner. I've changed the concept to enlisting allies, or battle buddies, in the fight for holiness.

The following paragraphs are adapted from Charles Swindoll's book *Dropping Your Guard*.[2]

1. **Allies must be both *honest and vulnerable*.** Both partners need to be open and transparent about all aspects of their lives. There is a risk of rejection in being unguarded and vulnerable, but this is essential. A true ally can't be bogus, phony, or counterfeit.

2. **Allies must be *available*.** My partner has to be available if and when I am struggling with temptation or when I need extra prayer reinforcement or need to be talked off the ledge. Mark Laaser in his book, *7 Principles of Highly Accountable Men* (Beacon Hill, 2011) said that each man requires at least seven or eight allies. If you call one man and the line is busy, then call the next man on your list. If he is not available, then keep working your way down the list. Undoubtedly, one of your allies will answer the phone.

3. **Allies must be *trustworthy*,** able to keep a secret, ready and willing to keep their mouths shut. If I hear a man gossip or slander or share things about another man that should have been held in confidence, I will never share my sin or weaknesses with that man. Proverbs 11:13 says, *"He who goes about as a talebearer reveals secrets, but he who is trustworthy and faithful in spirit keeps the matter hidden"* (AMPC).

4. **Allies must be *teachable*.** We must be willing to learn from each other. It requires humility to listen from the heart when a brother offers instruction.

In addition to these four traits, here are some other requirements for allies.

A good ally will not condemn you when sin is confessed. Rather he will grieve with you. There are enough shame and guilt already being heaped on you by Satan. You don't need more from someone else.

A good ally always points you back to Jesus, reminding you of the promises of forgiveness and offering hope. I went to Dave, one of my allies, because I knew I needed to confess some sin. I had looked at porn and masturbated (again). I felt miserable, weak, and useless before God. After Dave heard my confession, the first thing out of his mouth was, "It's been a long time since you've blown it. You are really growing!" He was genuine and excited. I was taken aback. I expected condemnation but received encouragement instead.

A good ally will ask hard questions. Stu was involved in a Bible study with four other guys. One week he confessed to the group, "I'm being hit on by another guy. Every time I go into the showers, this fellow also goes into the showers. He is offering me a sexual encounter, and I have resisted so far, but

---

[2] Adapted from Charles R. Swindoll, Dropping Your Guard (Waco, Texas, Word Books, 1983) page 172.

my flesh is weakening. Pray for strength." Over the course of the next five months, not one of those four guys asked Stu about his temptation. No one cared enough to risk asking the hard questions.

A good ally will not gloss over your sin. He will help you do a thorough post-sin analysis, asking questions such as, What circumstances were happening in your life that led you to sin? Were you stressed, tired, alone, bored, buzzed, or spiritually high? What pass did you give yourself that allowed your inner man to permit you to disobey God?

A good ally will project the trajectory of your sin, reminding you of its awful consequences. One man that I met with was an extroverted hugger. He would greet everyone, especially women, with a smile and a hug. We would meet at a downtown coffee shop and were constantly interrupted by people he knew. He was sanguine, and if there is a gift of greeting, he had it. But with one woman, the hug led to a kiss, which led to inappropriate touching. Over time, he confessed each step to me. Proverbs 2, 5, 6, 7, and 9 repeatedly point out the danger of such behavior. *"Surely her [the adulteress's] house leads down to death and her paths to the spirits of the dead. None who go to her return or attain the paths of life"* (Proverbs 2:18-19). He never consummated the relationship with this woman, but he came perilously close. He confessed this to his wife, and they are working through his infidelity. I had warned him repeatedly that he was on the wrong path. Even though he was blinded to the eventual outcome of his ways, I saw the trajectory that he was on and warned him repeatedly.

A good ally will pray for you and with you and enter into spiritual warfare with you, maybe even fasting with you and for you. A number of years ago, before the publication of my book *The War Within: Gaining Victory in the Battle for Sexual Purity*, I felt led by God to enter into a period of extended fasting. I knew that when the book was published, I'd come under more pressure and increased spiritual attacks. As I struggled with the decision to fast for forty days, a buddy said to me, "If you do that, I will do it with you." I couldn't believe that he would make such a commitment! So, for forty days, we encouraged, prayed for, and strengthened each other. He was, and still is, a true *ally*.

A good ally will help you think through tempting future situations. When you travel, he will ask you about your purity plan and maybe even take the initiative to call to check up on you when you are traveling.

A good ally will ask you, "Are you lying to me?" Eventually, he will know you well enough to tell if you are trying to hide, lie, or deceive.

How To Find An Ally

1. Pray fervently and ask God to give you an ally.

2. Choose men from your *Every Man A Pure Warrior* group or make a list of men that you know from church or Bible study groups, including pastors, relatives, and friends. Pray through each name asking the Lord for guidance.

3. Go to each man and discuss your search for and need of an ally.

4. Take the step of disclosing your struggles and your need for a true ally.

5. If you sense a kindred spirit, someone who readily empathizes with you, someone who divulges their own private struggles, then ask him if he would join you as a mutual ally in your common battle.

6. If you do NOT sense a kindred spirit, and the man says, "That's not my issue," or if you sense shame or rejection, or if you sense that he is NOT trustworthy, then move on to the next one on your list.

7. Be persistent in prayer and in asking men until the Lord gives you an ally.

How To Use An Ally

When a man is struggling with sexual temptation and wants help, the following is a checklist for using an ally.

1. Call a brother when you are tempted or have fallen.

2. Confess to your ally what you have done or feel tempted to do.

3. Pray a prayer of confession, asking God's forgiveness for the specific thing.

4. Begin to worship together. Pray through Psalm 103:8-12.

5. Sing or quote your favorite worship song.

6. Pray the Lord's Prayer together, personalizing it and naming your specific temptation. Focus on verse 13: "Lead us not into temptation, but deliver us from the evil one." Pray: **"Lord, deliver me from the tempter and his luring me to lust. Deliver me from the accuser and his non-stop name-calling."** Your ally should say, "I agree in the name of Jesus" when you are finished.

7. Your ally should pray, asking the Holy spirit to reveal what wounds or triggers have brought you to this temptation. Spend some time listening to what the Lord brings to mind. Then pray and extend forgiveness to the person who has hurt you. "Lord I extend forgiveness to _____ for _____."

8. Your ally will then ask if you have amputated, or thrown away, the item that caused you to be tempted. If it is a person, pray for his or her salvation or say a prayer of blessings.

9. Then take several minutes to quote three to five Scripture verses or passages you have memorized.

10. Preach two to three key aspects of the gospel message to yourself and thank the Lord for the truth of Romans 8:1. **"I thank You, Father, for the truth that there is no condemnation for those who are in Christ. Jesus, I thank You for dying on the cross for me. I praise You that I am forgiven. You look at me as if I had never sinned, and I am adopted into Your family. You purchased me, and now I am free from sin."**

You will need to repeat this process many times. Sometimes additional sins need to be confessed. Sometimes the Lord wants to reveal other people who have hurt you, to whom you need to extend forgiveness. This is a process. Our habits of yielding to sin and self-medicating were formed over time, and our healing will also be a process over time.

Follow the WWW A MAP Model to Guide You in Being a Good Ally.

The following six steps are on a perforated sheet at the back of the book. Tear it out and carry it with you until you learn these steps.

1. **Discuss worship**. Ask your brother, "How is your personal worship going?" Then spend some time worshiping together. Review portions of Psalm 103 or some other psalm that you've memorized and work through it verse by verse, praising and worshiping God.

   • Work through the skills of worship. Offer your body and your body parts to God as an act of worship. Mention specifically in prayer each body part involved in sin.

   • Review the words to your favorite song, hymn, psalm, or spiritual song. Worship God in the midst of the song.

   • Worship God by putting on the armor of God, mentioning each piece by name. Follow this by putting on the new nature, love, and Jesus.

2. **Discuss warfare**. Pray together the Lord's Prayer focusing on the holiness of God (verse 9) and lead us not into temptation (verse 13). Name the temptation, for example, watching porn, lust, masturbation, or something else. And focus on, deliver us from the Evil One. Name how you are being attacked: by temptation, by an accusation, by slander, or by other means, taking back the spiritual ground that was yielded to the Evil One.

3. **Move on to wounds**. What triggered you to sin? What wound was revealed through this sin? What inner needs were you seeking to meet? Come before God's throne, identifying the wound and asking God to both heal the wound and to help you forgive the person who caused the wound.

4. **Discuss the amputate step**. Ask about the delivery system for porn or whatever caused the sin. Ask: How are you going to disable or remove or eliminate the platform that is delivering sin to you?

5. **Next ask about their Scripture memory times and their review plans.** The battle for purity takes place in the mind. Review key Scriptures together.

6. **Close the WWW A MAP session by preaching and reviewing the gospel with each other**. Review the wonderful beauty of the sacrificial life, death and resurrection of Jesus. We are redeemed by the blood (Ephesians 1:7), are forgiven by the blood (Ephesians 1:7), are justified by the blood (Romans 5:9), are sanctified by the blood (Hebrews 13:12), and are being cleansed by the blood (1 John 1:7). Assure your friend that he is in fact forgiven (1 John 1:9, and James 5:16).

End in more worship, thanking God for the absolute cleansing and forgiveness of Jesus.

If you work through these steps, you are proving to be an ally in the struggle for holiness.

Remind your friend that he will be more vulnerable now that he has fallen. Satan will attack with guilt and shame and will attack God's promises by saying, "You are not forgiven." We must be on guard to resist these attacks after confession is made.

- ✓ **Leaders**: Divide the men into pairs. Have one man share the last time he blew it and needed to confess; have the other man act as the ally, and go through each of the WWW A MAP steps mentioned above. After they do this, have them switch roles.

- ✓ How would you describe the difference between being an ally and an accountability partner?

- ✓ Summarize the need for an ally. Keep in mind the difference between being an ally and an accountability partner.

✓ Lookup the following verses. Write down applicable principles for confronting and restoring a brother caught in sin.

Galatians 6:1-2

1 Thessalonians 5:14

Hebrews 3:13

ASSIGNMENT: Memorize Ecclesiastes 4:9-10.

Two are better than one, because they have a good return for their labor: If either of them falls down, one can help the other up. But pity anyone who falls and has no one to help them up. —ECCLESIASTES 4:9-10

✓ Meditate on Ecclesiastes 4:9-10, using the *Ask Questions* method. Jot down two or three thoughts.

✓ Rewrite Ecclesiastes 4:9-10 in your own words. Be prepared to share this with the group.

Ask Questions

Is there:

A command to obey

A promise to claim

A sin to avoid

An application to make

Something new about God

Ask: Who, What, When, Where, Why

Emphasize:
Different words

Rewrite
In your own words

Points to Remember

1. God does not want us to be loners. We each need battle buddies, allies, in our mutual pursuit for holiness. *"Pity the man who does not have an ally"* (Ecclesiastes 4:10).

2. Good allies are hard to find. If you don't have one, pray every day, asking God to give you at least one ally.

3. A good ally always points you back to Jesus, reminding you of the promises of Jesus and offering hope.

4. We are to fight for holiness *"along with those who call on the Lord out of a pure heart"* (2 Timothy 2:22).

5. WWW A MAP is a method of becoming a pure warrior and learning how to be an ally.

✓ To summarize this lesson, write out the most important things you learned.

✓ Record how many times this week you practiced WWW A MAP: _____

✓ **Leaders**: End the lesson by praying the WAR method of prayer.

Assignment for Next Week

1. In preparation for the next lesson, please have your Quiet Times this week in the following passages: Matthew 4:1-11, Romans 12:2, Ephesians 4:22-24, Proverbs 7:1-3, and Psalm 119:9-11. Take one verse or passage each day and meditate on it for your Quiet Times.

2. Try to record five to seven Quiet Times this week. It is okay to use one of your Quiet Times to complete the lesson and one to review verses and work on your current verse.

3. Practice the WAR method of prayer in your Quiet Times this week. Continue praying for the men in your group to have consistent and quality times with the Lord. Pray against the Enemy's attacking the Quiet Times of the men in the group.

4. Place Ecclesiastes 4:9-10 in the front window of your verse pack and memorize it this week.

5. Finish any lessons that you have not completed.

6. Be prepared to share all your *Every Man A Pure Warrior* verses.

7. Read through and complete next week's lesson.

8. Every day, practice WWW A MAP. At least once this week, call your ally and ask him how he is doing in the battle for purity. Use WWW A MAP as a guideline.

ALLIES: BATTLE BUDDIES

Worship

- Start worshiping God by praising Him. Sing your favorite hymn, psalm, or worship song. Offer your body and body parts to God as an act of worship and clothe your body with the armor of God.

Warfare Praying

- First, confess any known sin by praying and say the following spiritual warfare prayer. "Lord Jesus, I ask forgiveness for _____ [name any sin that comes to mind such as looking at porn, masturbation, lust, anger, unforgiveness, greed, or hate]."
- Pray the Lord's Prayer: "Our Father in heaven, hallowed be your name, your kingdom come, your will be done, on earth as it is in heaven. Give us today our daily bread, and forgive us our debts, as we also have forgiven our debtors. And lead us not into temptation, but deliver us from the evil one, for yours is the kingdom and the power and the glory forever. Amen" (Matthew 6:9-13).
- After praying the prayer, personalize it for your temptation. "Lord, please deliver me from the Tempter who is tempting me to _____. Lord, please deliver me from the Accuser who is telling me that my sin is not forgiven." If you are praying with a partner, the partner should say, "I agree in the name of Jesus."

Wounds and Triggers

- Ask the Holy Spirit to show you any wounds that are causing you to act out. Extend forgiveness to anyone who has hurt you. "Lord, I extend forgiveness to _____ for _____."

Amputate

- Separate yourself from any source of porn or lust-inducing environments. If you have just seen a pretty woman who is triggering you, begin to pray for her salvation, that she would find Christ and walk with Him.

Memorize Scripture

- Review your Scripture verses. Begin quoting out loud the verses from Psalm 103, Romans 6, EMAW verses, or any other memorized passages of Scripture.

Allies

- Call a brother for prayer when tempted, confess if you have blown it, and begin to go through these seven principles together.

Preach the Gospel to Yourself Daily

- "I thank You, Father, for the truth that 'there is now no condemnation for those who are in Christ Jesus' (Romans 8:1). I thank You, Jesus, for dying on the cross for me. I praise You that I am forgiven. You look at me as if I had never sinned, and I am adopted into Your family. You purchased me, and now I am free from sin."

WWW A MAP SEVEN KEYS TO FREEDOM

TRY Covenant Eyes Today!

Sign up at **covenanteyes.com** with the promo code: EMAPW. And get the first 30 days for FREE.

How it Works
choose an ally • take your life back • accountability for men and women

01. choose
You choose a trusted friend to be your Ally and set realistic goals to start moving forward.

02. monitor
Covenant Eyes monitors all your screens for porn. If it's detected, we alert your Ally by sending blurred screenshots of the activity to them in an emailed report. Covenant Eyes today!

03. connect
You and your Ally have honest conversations about your struggle, your triggers, and how to keep moving forward.

04. live
In time, porn loses its power over your life and you leave it behind. You can finally live in freedom.

LESSON 4
SCRIPTURE MEMORY: KEY TO TRANSFORMATION

✓ Have the men break into pairs and recite all their *Every Man A Pure Warrior* verses to each other. Have one man hold the cards and say the reference while the other man quotes the verse and says the reference at the end of the verse. Then have them switch roles.

✓ Sign off on the *Completion Records*.

✓ Open the session with prayer.

✓ Go around the room, asking each man to share one Quiet Time.

✓ Begin reading the lesson paragraph by paragraph.

✓ Depending on time, have as many men as possible share their *Ask Questions*, meditations and their rewrites of Romans 12:2 and Psalm 119:9-11.

✓ Read the *Points to Remember* and the *Assignment*.

✓ Break into pairs and practice WWW A MAP with each other. After one man works through it, have them reverse the roles.

This lesson will focus on four equally important reasons to memorize Scripture: (1) the sufficiency of God's Word for memory washing, (2) the need to have the spiritual weapons to fight against a spiritual enemy, (3) the certainty of God's promises and warnings, and (4) the Word's role in our spiritual transformation.

Washing: Chris's Story

Chris loved porn. His mom and dad divorced when he was a newborn, and he never met his dad. When he was ten, his mom bought him a subscription to a pornographic magazine. When she gave him the first magazine, she explained about the biology of sex, taught him how to masturbate, and told him it was better to touch himself than to touch girls. He soon graduated to spending hours surfing internet porn.

But then, Chris was invited by a girl to attend her church youth group. Chris was intrigued by the stories of Jesus. After several months of reading the Gospels, he came under the conviction of sin and gave his life to Jesus Christ. Soon after that, Chris sought me out for help to become a real disciple of Jesus. He said, "I want to grow. I got rid of my porn, but I have so much junk stuck in my head that I can't think of anything but porn. Can you help me?"

I told Chris, "I can and will help you, but it will cost you. It will cost you time and effort and dedication. If you want to grow in this area, you must learn how to take control of your thought life." I asked him, "Are you willing to spend as much time memorizing and meditating on Scripture as you spent consuming porn?" And he agreed to start the discipling process.

- ✓ How can our brains be cleansed from the stain of porn? Lookup the following passages: John 15:3, Ephesians 5:25-27, and 1 John 1:7.

✓ How often do you experience flashbacks or images from past sexual sin?

✓ What price will you have to pay to cleanse your brain? Are you willing to spend half the time you used to spend pursuing porn on memorizing Scripture?

Weapons

Jesus had God's Word memorized. He was able to immediately, with the Holy Spirit's help, quote the Scripture He needed to counter temptation. Jesus modeled for us how the memorized Word is a powerful spiritual weapon that we need in our combat with the Evil One.

We live in a hostile environment saturated with porn. Satan has declared war on us. We need spiritual weapons to fight a spiritual, unseen enemy. Another key reason to memorize Scriptures is to acquire the necessary spiritual weapons to fight an unseen enemy and win this battle successfully.

✓ Read the story of the temptation of Christ as found in Luke 4:1-13 and Matthew 4:1-11. In preparation for the ministry, Jesus fasted for forty days. *"Then Jesus was led by the Spirit into the wilderness to be tempted by the devil"* (Matthew 4:1). When Satan launched his attack, he preyed on the fact that Jesus was hungry.

Jesus responded by quoting Deuteronomy 8:3: *"It is written: 'Man shall not live on bread alone, but on every word that comes from the mouth of God'"* (Matthew 4:4).

This method was not lost on Satan. In round two of this battle, Satan misquoted Scripture in an attempt to get Jesus to commit suicide. Jesus did not deviate from his practice of quoting Scripture to defeat temptation and Satan.

Satan again tempted Jesus by offering all the kingdoms of the world to Him. For the third time, Jesus quoted Scripture, this time Deuteronomy 6:13.

How long does it take for a person to sin in his thinking sexually? How long does it take for an image to be seen before it's lusted over? Since we can sin in a mere fraction of a second, we need to have weapons that can be deployed equally quickly. The only way to be equipped for temptation and assault is to have spiritual weapons always ready. Satan's flaming arrows can quickly ignite into more and more impure thoughts that will inevitably lead to impure actions unless we immediately put out the fire.

Memorizing Scripture is not optional for a spiritual warrior. We must memorize and meditate on Scripture. This allows us to understand and obey the principles in order to have powerful, spiritual weapons to use against our invisible, deceitful, spiritual enemy. We don't fight against flesh and blood; worldly, fleshly weapons won't work against demons. We must have spiritual weapons to fight against a spiritual foe. By memorizing Scripture, you arm yourself with spiritual weapons.

✓ Lookup Deuteronomy 6:6-7 and Joshua 1:8. How do these two passages relate to Scripture memory?

"Bible memorization is absolutely fundamental to spiritual formation. If I had to choose between all the disciplines of the spiritual life, I would choose Bible memorization, because it is a fundamental way of filling our minds with what it needs. This book of the law shall not depart out of your mouth. That's where you need it! How does it get in your mouth? Memorization." —Dallas Willard

✓ Do you believe this quote? Why or why not?

✓ Read the following verses and describe the weapons mentioned.

2 Corinthians 10:3-5

Hebrews 4:12-13

Promises and Warnings

Promises from God are statements of factual, spiritual truth that are entirely trustworthy. We can rely on them, believe in them, and trust them. The promises of God reflect the very nature of God, who is faithful and true. When God says that something is going to happen, we can trust that it most assuredly will!

- ✓ Another reason to hide God's Word in your heart is found in Philippians 4:8-9. Look it up and describe the connection between purity and the promises of God.

- ✓ Lookup 1 Corinthians 4:5 and Hebrews 13:4. What promises and warnings are mentioned regarding sexual sin?

- ✓ How can the promises and warnings of God help us with the process of perfecting holiness in our lives? (2 Corinthians 7:1)

✓ Lookup some of the promises of God that have helped many in the pursuit of holiness. Note whether they are conditional, and if so, what condition must we meet to receive something from God?

1 John 1:9

James 4:7-10

Transformation

As I met with Chris, he was memorizing new Scriptures each week and learning to meditate on them; he was in the process of being transformed. He was changing. Instead of going throughout the day having impure thoughts and sexual images popping into his head every few minutes, now he had the Word of God in his head. The Holy Spirit was using the Word of God to change his attitude about women, life, himself, and God. The Word was changing his values.

Once you have been exposed to pornography, you cannot become and stay pure unless you memorize massive amounts of Scripture. This is mandatory. Verses hidden in our hearts become the basis of comfort and hope and give us the weapons needed to win the war against our souls.

✓ How does Scripture memory change your attitude and your actions with women, life, and God?

Transformation comes from the renewing of our minds with God's Word. Know this: Control your thoughts, and you can control your behavior.

Dr. Howard Hendricks of Dallas Theological Seminary once said that if it were his decision, every graduate would be required to learn one thousand verses, word-perfect.

Assignment 1: Romans 12:2.

Do not conform to the pattern of this world, but be transformed by the renewing of your mind. Then you will be able to test and approve what God's will is—his good, pleasing and perfect will.
—Romans 12:2

✓ Meditate on Romans 12:2, using the *Ask Questions* method. Jot down two or three thoughts.

> **Ask Questions**
>
> **Is there:**
>
> A command to obey
>
> A promise to claim
>
> A sin to avoid
>
> An application to make
>
> Something new about God
>
> Ask: Who, What, When, Where, Why
>
> **Emphasize:**
> Different words
>
> **Rewrite**
> In your own words

✓ Rewrite Romans 12:2 in your own words. Be prepared to share this with the group.

Assignment 2: Memorize Psalm 119:9-11.

How can a young person stay on the path of purity? By living according to your word. I seek you with all my heart; do not let me stray from your commands. I have hidden your word in my heart that I might not sin against you.
—Psalm 119:9-11

✓ Meditate on Psalm 119:9-11, using the *Ask Questions* method. Jot down two or three thoughts.

✓ Rewrite Psalm 119:9-11 in your own words. Be prepared to share this with the group.

Points to Remember

1. Jesus demonstrated that we cannot fight Satan without hiding God's Word in our hearts. God's Word is a supernatural cleansing agent that will rebuild and purify our porn-poisoned minds.

2. God's Word is a powerful spiritual weapon. We need to arm ourselves with the weapons of God's Word to be effective, equipped spiritual warriors.

3. Scripture memory and meditation, with obedience, will lead to spiritual transformation.

4. Scripture memory is hard work requiring discipline and consistency, but through grace and the help of the Holy Spirit, it can be done. It also helps to have a buddy to spur us on.

✓ To summarize this lesson, write out the most important things you learned.

✓ Record how many times this week you practiced WWW A MAP:
_____

✓ **Leaders**: Have the men break into pairs and practice WWW A MAP. Follow the model on pages 36–37. After one man works through it, have them reverse roles.

ASSIGNMENT FOR NEXT WEEK

1. Aim for five to seven Quiet Times this week. Use these psalms: Psalm 103, Psalm 99, and Psalm 145.

2. Dedicate at least one Quiet Time this week to hymns and spiritual songs. Focus on pouring out your heart to God in worshipful music.

3. Practice the WAR method of prayer in your Quiet Times this week. Continue praying for the men in your group to have consistent quality times with the Lord. Pray against the Enemy's attacking the Quiet Times of the men in the group.

4. Place Romans 12:2 in the front window of your verse pack and memorize it this week. If you already have this verse memorized, then place Psalm 119:9-11 in the verse pack window and start learning it.

5. Finish any lessons that you have not completed.

6. Be prepared to share all your Every Man A Pure Warrior verses.

7. Read through and complete next week's lesson.

8. Every day, practice WWW A MAP. At least once this week call a member of your group and ask him how he is doing in the battle for purity. Use WWW A MAP as a guideline.

Worship

- Start worshiping God by praising Him. Sing your favorite hymn, psalm, or worship song. Offer your body and body parts to God as an act of worship and clothe your body with the armor of God.

Warfare Praying

- First, confess any known sin by praying and say the following spiritual warfare prayer. "Lord Jesus, I ask forgiveness for _____ [name any sin that comes to mind such as looking at porn, masturbation, lust, anger, unforgiveness, greed, or hate]."

- Pray the Lord's Prayer: "Our Father in heaven, hallowed be your name, your kingdom come, your will be done, on earth as it is in heaven. Give us today our daily bread, and forgive us our debts, as we also have forgiven our debtors. And lead us not into temptation, but deliver us from the evil one, for yours is the kingdom and the power and the glory forever. Amen" (Matthew 6:9-13).

- After praying the prayer, personalize it for your temptation. "Lord, please deliver me from the Tempter who is tempting me to _____. Lord, please deliver me from the Accuser who is telling me that my sin is not forgiven." If you are praying with a partner, the partner should say, "I agree in the name of Jesus."

Wounds and Triggers

- Ask the Holy Spirit to show you any wounds that are causing you to act out. Extend forgiveness to anyone who has hurt you. "Lord, I extend forgiveness to _____ for _____."

Amputate

- Separate yourself from any source of porn or lust-inducing environments. If you have just seen a pretty woman who is triggering you, begin to pray for her salvation, that she would find Christ and walk with Him.

Memorize Scripture

- Review your Scripture verses. Begin quoting out loud the verses from Psalm 103, Romans 6, EMAW verses, or any other memorized passages of Scripture.

Allies

- Call a brother for prayer when tempted, confess if you have blown it, and begin to go through these seven principles together.

Preach the Gospel to Yourself Daily

- "I thank You, Father, for the truth that 'there is now no condemnation for those who are in Christ Jesus' (Romans 8:1). I thank You, Jesus, for dying on the cross for me. I praise You that I am forgiven. You look at me as if I had never sinned, and I am adopted into Your family. You purchased me, and now I am free from sin."

LESSON 5
AGGRESSIVE WORSHIP SKILL 1: MEMORIZE PSALM 103:8-12

✓ Have the men break into pairs and recite all their *Every Man A Pure Warrior* verses to each other, beginning with Romans 12:2 and Psalm 119:9-11. Have one man hold the cards and say the reference while the other man quotes the verses and says the reference at the end of the passage.

✓ Ask, "How did each of you do this week in practicing WWW A MAP?"

✓ Sign off on the *Completion Records*.

✓ Open the session with prayer.

✓ Go around the room, asking each man to share one Quiet Time.

✓ Begin reading the lesson paragraph by paragraph.

✓ Depending on time, have as many men as possible share their *Ask Questions*, meditations, and rewrites of Psalm 103:8-12.

✓ Read the *Points to Remember* and the *Assignment*.

✓ Break into pairs and practice WWW A MAP with each other. After one man works through it, have them reverse the roles.

Aggressive Worship is the First of Seven Principles That Must Be Mastered in Overcoming Enslavement to Sexual Sin. We Must Learn to be Aggressive Worshipers of the Living God.

Enjoying God: Bob's Story

My parents divorced when I was ten years old. Shortly after my dad left our house, some neighborhood boys showed me pornography and invited me to join their "coming of age" club. The boys all had girlie magazines stolen from their dads' porn stashes. We all got naked and touched each other. It was there that I first heard about the birds and the bees, learned to masturbate, and developed ungodly attitudes and worldly views about men, women, sex, and marriage.

I gave my life to Jesus in high school; no one was there to help me grow in the faith. After my freshman year in college, I met a group of Christians who taught me how to walk with God. I learned almost all the principles found in the first Every Man A Warrior book. I learned the disciplines and importance of memorizing Scripture, how to have a Quiet Time, how to meditate, and how to apply Scriptures.

But the things that I had not learned were how to worship God, how to delight in God, or how to love God. I missed the heart connection of the Great Commandment found in Matthew 22:36-37, *"to love the Lord with all my heart, soul, mind, and strength."*

I missed the whole reason for each of the disciplines. If I had my Quiet Time, memorized a verse, had an application, or shared the gospel with someone, then I felt that God would love me. Everything that I did was performance based. If I didn't do any of the disciplines, I was sure that I had blown it for the day, that God would not listen to my prayers, and that God was disappointed in me. I was trying to earn His love. Since God is God—pure, holy, infinite, and perfect—I was continually trying to be perfect but never measuring up. Consequently, I felt guilt and shame all day. Everything I did, no matter how hard I tried or how perfect I thought it was, was never enough for this perfect God. I was also continually comparing myself with other believers around me, who seemed to always be doing more or doing it better than I was. These thoughts led to more guilt, more shame.

I expressed all these thoughts to my mentor. After listening to me, he put his finger on part of the problem. He said, "You are approaching God like He is a computer. You think that if you do all these things, then God will love you and accept you." He looked at me and lovingly said, "You can't earn God's love. He already loves you. You can't perform enough to be acceptable to God. Jesus did all that when He died on the cross. *Your problem is that you don't know how to enjoy God. You don't know how to worship God. You don't know how to get out of yourself and get lost in the greatness of God.*"

It is true: I had not learned to enjoy God.

✓ How do you feel about Bob's story?

✓ How do you feel about the following Tim Keller quote?

If you are a Christian and you are dealing with enslaving habits, it's not enough to say, 'Bad Christian, stop it.' And it is not enough to beat yourself up or merely try harder and harder and harder... The secret to freedom from enslaving patterns of sin is worship. You need worship. You need great worship... And this needs to be happening all the time.

—Tim Keller, from the sermon "Sin as Slavery"

✓ How do we stop trying to earn God's love through spiritual disciplines, and just enjoy his love?

My mentor then gave me an assignment. He told me to memorize an entire psalm. He suggested Psalm 103. Then he taught me to pray through it, using each verse as a springboard to worship God. He was very clear. He said, "Most men don't know how to worship God. Worship is praising God for who He is and thanking Him for what He has done. Unfortunately for many, thanksgiving can quickly become me-centered. We end up thinking about how God gave me something or did something for me, and then the focus subtly shifts away from God." The requirements of this study are to memorize only verses 8-12 of Psalm 103. However, I encourage you to memorize the entire psalm!

✓ **Leaders**: Starting with Psalm 103:8, have each person read one verse of the psalm. Focus on one of the attributes of God that the psalm highlights and spend time in prayer, worshiping God for who He is. For verse 8, mention some of the things a person might vocalize in worship. Continue with your group, in this process until you've prayed and worshiped through Psalm 103:8-12.

"The Lord is compassionate and gracious, slow to anger, abounding in love."
—Psalm 103:8

Father, I praise You for your kindness and compassion toward me. I worship You, adore You, and praise You that You are slow to anger and that You love me with overflowing love.

✓ Come up with similar prayers for the following verses.

"He will not always accuse, nor will he harbor his anger forever."
—Psalm 103:9

"He does not treat us as our sins deserve or repay us according to our iniquities." —Psalm 103:10

"For as high as the heavens are above the earth, so great is his love for those who fear him." —Psalm 103:11

"As far as the east is from the west, so far has he removed our transgressions from us." —Psalm 103:12

This was the first psalm that I memorized. There are so many *great* truths about God recorded here by one of the premier worshipers in the history of the world, King David.

I memorized the psalm because of the facts found that apply specifically to the quest for purity.

- ✓ Read through Psalm 103 and list at least five attributes, or characteristics, of God, found in this psalm and how they apply to the battle for purity.

Connecting our Lack of Worship with Sexual Sin.

- ✓ Lookup Romans 1:18-32. List five expectations that God has for us as humans created by Him.

- ✓ When we fail to worship God, fail to glorify Him as God, fail to give thanks to Him, fail to serve Him, or even refuse to remember Him, what are the horrible consequences of our failure to worship?

You worship your way into an addiction, and you must worship your way out of an addiction.

—Adapted from John Avant, *If God Were Real: A Journey Into a Faith That Matters*

✓ Based on Romans 1:18-32, why do you think our failure to worship God leads to sexual sin?

✓ Lookup Revelation 5 and read it. How does this chapter model "aggressive worship"? What is the object of worship? What words are used; what postures taken?

As I was driving to work the other day, I got hit with an impure thought. There was a sudden desire to look for and find pornography and then act out all the sexual sin that follows impure thinking. I couldn't figure out the source of the impure thought. Several minutes later I was hit again with another temptation. It dawned on me that I was under attack. Drawing on my years of training, I knew that the most important thing was to engage in *aggressive, heartfelt worship*.

The first step on the list is to engage in aggressive, heartfelt worship. I quickly started quoting Psalm 103, and after each verse or phrase, I verbalized worship and praise toward God. The invitation to lust was the world calling me to worship my flesh. I had a choice: worshiping my flesh by lusting, consuming porn, and masturbating, or worshiping God through heartfelt praise and adoration. I chose God. As I worshiped, the temptation died away. In the battle for sexual purity, we *must* learn how to be aggressive worshipers of the living God.

ASSIGNMENT: Memorize Psalm 103:8-12.

The Lord is compassionate and gracious, slow to anger, abounding in love. He will not always accuse, nor will he harbor his anger forever; he does not treat us as our sins deserve or repay us according to our iniquities. For as high as the heavens are above the earth, so great is his love for those who fear him; as far as the east is from the west, so far has he removed our transgressions from us. —Psalm 103:8-12

✓ Meditate on Psalm 103:8-12, using the *Ask Questions* method. Jot down two or three thoughts.

✓ For future development in learning how to worship aggressively, consider memorizing Colossians 1:15-20 and Philippians 2:5-10. These great passages focus on the beauty and glory of Christ our Savior.

Ask Questions

Is there:

A command to obey

A promise to claim

A sin to avoid

An application to make

Something new about God

Ask: Who, What, When, Where, Why

Emphasize:
Different words

Rewrite
In your own words

Points to Remember

1. Every temptation to gratify the flesh is a call to worship the flesh. We must choose to use this as a springboard to instead worship God.

2. One effective way to worship God is to quote a psalm and after each verse or phrase verbalize praise and worship for God, extolling the attributes mentioned in the psalm.

3. The first step in overcoming enslavement to sexual sin is to learn to be an aggressive worshiper of God.

✓ To summarize this lesson, write out the most important things you learned.

✓ Record how many times this week you practiced WWW A MAP:
_____

✓ **Leaders**: Have the men break into pairs and practice WWW A MAP with each other. Follow the model found on pages 36–37. After one man works through it, have them reverse roles.

Assignment for Next Week

1. Try to record five to seven Quiet Times this week in the following passages: Psalm 33:1-3, Psalm 92:1-3, 2 Chronicles 20:1-30, and Matthew 26:26-30. It is okay to use one of your Quiet Times to complete the lesson and another to review verses and memorize the psalm.

2. Practice worshiping God by praying through verses 8-12 of Psalm 103.

3. Place Psalm 103:8-12 in the front window of your verse pack and memorize it this week. If you are ambitious, try memorizing the whole psalm. Print it and carry it with you, reading through it five to ten times per day. Read and quote it at night as you go to sleep. Saturate your mind with this psalm. It may take two to three weeks to have it memorized.

4. Finish any lessons that you have not completed.

5. Complete next week's lesson and come ready to share your answers with the group.

6. Be prepared to share all your *Every Man A Pure Warrior* verses.

7. Every day, go through WWW A MAP. Practice each of the seven steps.

WWW A MAP — SEVEN KEYS TO FREEDOM

Worship
- Start worshiping God by praising Him. Sing your favorite hymn, psalm, or worship song. Offer your body and body parts to God as an act of worship and clothe your body with the armor of God.

Warfare Praying
- First, confess any known sin by praying and say the following spiritual warfare prayer. "Lord Jesus, I ask forgiveness for _____ [name any sin that comes to mind such as looking at porn, masturbation, lust, anger, unforgiveness, greed, or hate]."
- Pray the Lord's Prayer: "Our Father in heaven, hallowed be your name, your kingdom come, your will be done, on earth as it is in heaven. Give us today our daily bread, and forgive us our debts, as we also have forgiven our debtors. And lead us not into temptation, but deliver us from the evil one, for yours is the kingdom and the power and the glory forever. Amen" (Matthew 6:9-13).
- After praying the prayer, personalize it for your temptation. "Lord, please deliver me from the Tempter who is tempting me to _____. Lord, please deliver me from the Accuser who is telling me that my sin is not forgiven." If you are praying with a partner, the partner should say, "I agree in the name of Jesus."

Wounds and Triggers
- Ask the Holy Spirit to show you any wounds that are causing you to act out. Extend forgiveness to anyone who has hurt you. "Lord, I extend forgiveness to_____ for _____."

Amputate
- Separate yourself from any source of porn or lust-inducing environments. If you have just seen a pretty woman who is triggering you, begin to pray for her salvation, that she would find Christ and walk with Him.

Memorize Scripture
- Review your Scripture verses. Begin quoting out loud the verses from Psalm 103, Romans 6, EMAW verses, or any other memorized passages of Scripture.

Allies
- Call a brother for prayer when tempted, confess if you have blown it, and begin to go through these seven principles together.

Preach the Gospel to Yourself Daily
- "I thank You, Father, for the truth that 'there is now no condemnation for those who are in Christ Jesus' (Romans 8:1). I thank You, Jesus, for dying on the cross for me. I praise You that I am forgiven. You look at me as if I had never sinned, and I am adopted into Your family. You purchased me, and now I am free from sin."

LESSON 6
Aggressive Worship Skill 2: Singing Psalms, Hymns, and Spiritual Songs

✓ Have the men break into pairs and recite all their Every Man A Pure Warrior verses to each other, beginning with Psalm 103:8-12. Have one man hold the cards and say the reference while the other man quotes the verses and says the reference at the end of the passage.

✓ Sign off on the *Completion Records*.

✓ Open the session with prayer.

✓ Go around the room, asking each man to share one Quiet Time.

✓ Begin reading the lesson paragraph by paragraph.

✓ Depending on time, have as many men as possible share their *Ask Questions*, meditations, and their favorite inspirational song.

✓ Read the *Points to Remember* and the *Assignment* for the next meeting.

✓ Break into pairs and practice WWW A MAP with each other. After one man works through it, have them reverse the roles.

THIS LESSON EXPLAINS FURTHER HOW TO BECOME AGGRESSIVE WORSHIPERS OF THE LIVING GOD, THROUGH THE SINGING OF PSALMS, HYMNS, AND SPIRITUAL SONGS.

GOD THE MUSICIAN

In my pit of darkness, every day that I opened the Scriptures, I felt condemnation and judgment. I was not enjoying God, and my Quiet Times were dry. Somehow I needed to change things up and get refreshed and revive my relationship with God.

When I turned on the radio and tuned the dial to a Christian radio station, a song started playing that pierced my hardness of heart and enlightened my eyes. It was a song called "East to West" by the group Casting Crowns, and some of the lyrics were straight out of Psalm 103. Somehow the Scriptures put to music became life-giving to my soul. This song and many others have revived me, keeping me from sin and helping me refocus on God.

- ✓ **Leaders**: If you've never heard this song before, search YouTube for Casting Crowns, "East to West".

- ✓ Yet another time I was wandering and becoming convinced that my sins were unforgivable. Another song played on the radio and the lyrics sang truth to my soul. Read these lyrics, focusing on the third verse.

    ***It Is Well With My Soul*[3]**

    When peace like a river, attendeth my way,
    When sorrows like sea billows roll
    Whatever my lot, thou hast taught me to say
    It is well, it is well, with my soul

    Chorus:
    It is well
    With my soul
    It is well, it is well with my soul

    Though Satan should buffet, though trials should come,
    Let this blest assurance control,
    That Christ has regarded my helpless estate,
    And hath shed His own blood for my soul. [Repeat Chorus]

AGGRESSIVE WORSHIP SKILL 2: SINGING PSALMS, HYMNS AND SPIRITUAL SONGS

My sin, oh, the bliss of this glorious thought
My sin, not in part but the whole,
Is nailed to the cross, and I bear it no more,
Praise the Lord, praise the Lord, o my soul. [Repeat Chorus Twice]

After hearing this song, I immediately downloaded it and played it over and over, memorizing both the tune and the lyrics. The Scriptural truths put in musical form penetrated into the depths of my soul. I found myself singing it throughout the day; it reminded me that I was indeed forgiven. God was telling me that the sins that always seemed to be so close were really far from me and that all my sins were forgiven.

Let the message of Christ dwell among you richly as you teach and admonish one another with all wisdom through psalms, hymns, and songs from the Spirit, singing to God with gratitude in your hearts.
—Colossians 3:16

King David was a masterful musician and songwriter. The word psalm means "song." Forty-two different psalms urge us to "sing to the LORD."

✓ Lookup the following verses and note the connection between singing and worship.

Psalm 33:1-3

Psalm 92:1-3

Singing songs of praise and worship is not just a beautiful thing to do: it is indispensable as a weapon of warfare. Psalm 22:3 says, *"Thou art holy, enthroned on the praises of Israel"* (RSV).

Imagine the following scenario. As an army commander, you know that a superior force is marching toward you and your troops. The king cried out to God for help. God promises the king that *"the battle is not yours but God's"* 2 Chronicles 20:15 (RSVCE). So in response to God's promise of victory,

---
[3] It is Well With My Soul written by Horatio Spafford in 1876; now in the public domain.

your strategy for attacking and winning this battle is not sending your most skilled, veteran fighters to the front lines but instead finding out who the best singers are in your ranks and sending them. Unbelievable? Think again.

> **I believe truly that Satan cannot endure it and so slips out of the room— more or less— when there is a true song.**
>
> —Amy Carmichael

✓ Read 2 Chronicles 20:1-30. Note the role of singing in winning the battle against Moab and the Ammonites.

✓ Read Matthew 26:26-30. What was the last thing Jesus and His disciples did together during the Last Supper?

✓ Read Acts 16:24-26 and note the singing before Apostle Paul's release from jail. Why do you think Paul and Silas were singing in this unlikely place?

King Saul started out well. He had been chosen by God to be the first earthly king of Israel. But because of Saul's willful disobedience and lack of faith, God rejected him as king. After the rejection, an evil spirit came upon Saul.

✓ Read the following account from 1 Samuel 16:14-23. Note the connection of David playing the lyre and Saul getting relief from an evil spirit.

AGGRESSIVE WORSHIP SKILL 2: SINGING PSALMS, HYMNS AND SPIRITUAL SONGS

Now the Spirit of the LORD had departed from Saul, and an evil spirit from the LORD tormented him.

Saul's attendants said to him, "See, an evil spirit from God is tormenting you. Let our lord command his servants here to search for someone who can play the lyre. He will play when the evil spirit from God comes on you, and you will feel better."

So, Saul said to his attendants, "Find someone who plays well and bring him to me."

One of the servants answered, "I have seen a son of Jesse of Bethlehem who knows how to play the lyre. He is a brave man and a warrior. He speaks well and is a fine-looking man. And the LORD is with him."

Then Saul sent messengers to Jesse and said, "Send me your son David, who is with the sheep." So, Jesse took a donkey loaded with bread, a skin of wine, and a young goat and sent them with his son David to Saul.

David came to Saul and entered his service. Saul liked him very much, and David became one of his armor-bearers. Then Saul sent word to Jesse, saying, "Allow David to remain in my service, for I am pleased with him."

Whenever the spirit from God came on Saul, David would take up his lyre and play. Then relief would come to Saul; he would feel better, and the evil spirit would leave him.

—1 SAMUEL 16:14-23

> The example from the life of David illustrates a practice I have: singing worship songs or having worship songs playing helps me keep in a state of continual worship, focusing on the greatness of God's goodness, mercy, and love.

I had fallen again into the pit of porn, lust, and masturbation. Every day was a battle, and I was losing most days. My traditional Quiet Times didn't seem to be helping. I live near the ocean and would simply get up early in the morning and walk along the beach. I did not take my Bible; instead, I took a hymnal. I would pick a hymn that I was familiar with and sing it out loud. Fortunately, the crashing of the waves would drown out my voice, and since it was around dawn, only a few scattered fishermen were at the beach, spread out every five hundred yards or so. I came to John Newton's great hymn "Amazing Grace" and sang all the verses. I sang it again and again. Every day for several weeks, my entire Quiet Time was spent singing this great hymn aloud.

It deeply ministered to me. All the lyrics are Scripture-based nuggets of truth. As I would sing it over and over, it became a prayer. As it penetrated my soul and lodged in my memory banks, I would not only sing but also pray the lyrics. It gave me inner strength and power. It renewed and revived my soul and made me feel connected to God.

✓ Read the following selection from "Amazing Grace." Underline any truth that speaks to your heart.

> *Amazing grace! How sweet the sound,*
> *That saved a wretch like me.*
> *I once was lost, but now am found,*
> *Was blind, but now I see.*
>
> *'Twas grace that taught my heart to fear,*
> *And grace my fears relieved;*
> *How precious did that grace appear,*
> *The hour I first believed!*
>
> *Through many dangers, toils and snares,*
> *I have already come;*
> *'Tis grace has brought me safe thus far,*
> *And grace will lead me home.*
>
> *When we've been there ten thousand years,*
> *Bright shining as the sun,*
> *We've no less days to sing God's praise*
> *Than when we first begun.*

ASSIGNMENT: Read or sing the hymn "Amazing Grace" again and again until you memorize the words to this great song of faith. If this song is unfamiliar to you, substitute a different one of your choice. It needs to be a song that focuses on God's attributes, such as His character, His might, or His love.

✓ Meditate on the words of "Amazing Grace" (or the hymn or song you choose to memorize), using the Ask Questions method. Jot down two or three thoughts.

> **Ask Questions**
>
> **Is there:**
>
> A command to obey
>
> A promise to claim
>
> A sin to avoid
>
> An application to make
>
> Something new about God
>
> Ask: Who, What, When, Where, Why
>
> **Emphasize:**
> Different words
>
> **Rewrite**
> In your own words

✓ What song, psalm, or hymn has profoundly impacted you, helped you think of God during a time of spiritual need, or brought you into God's presence? Share the song with the group, or have it queued up beforehand.

Points to Remember

1. Singing songs of worship and praise is a weapon in our arsenal.

2. We are commanded to teach and admonish one another in psalms, hymns, and spiritual songs.

3. Music draws us into the presence of God and gives us confidence in our fight against evil.

✓ To summarize this lesson, write out the most important things you learned.

✓ Record how many times this week you practiced WWW A MAP: _____

✓ **Leaders**: Have the men break into pairs and practice WWW A MAP with each other. Follow the model found on pages 36–37. After one man works through it, have them reverse roles.

Assignment for Next Week

1. Start your Quiet Times every day this week singing the song "Amazing Grace" or a different worship song of your choice. Reflect on the words as you sing. Make the hymn a meditation.

2. Try to record five to seven Quiet Times this week from either the hymn "Amazing Grace," the hymn or song that you choose, or any of the following passages: Romans 12:1, Romans 6:11-14, and Psalm 5:1-3. It is okay to use one of your Quiet Times to complete the lesson and one to review verses and work on memorizing this hymn.

3. Practice worshiping God by praying through each verse or phrase of Psalm 103:8-12.

4. Place "Amazing Grace" in the front window of your verse pack and memorize it this week. If you have chosen another hymn or song, write it out and then place it in your verse pack.

5. Finish any lessons that you have not completed.

6. Be prepared to share all your Every Man A Pure Warrior verses.

7. Study the next lesson, answering all the questions, and be ready to share your insights next week with your group.

8. Every day, go through WWW A MAP. Practice each of the seven steps.

AGGRESSIVE WORSHIP SKILL 2: SINGING PSALMS, HYMNS AND SPIRITUAL SONGS

Worship

- Start worshiping God by praising Him. Sing your favorite hymn, psalm, or worship song. Offer your body and body parts to God as an act of worship and clothe your body with the armor of God.

Warfare Praying

- First, confess any known sin by praying and say the following spiritual warfare prayer. "Lord Jesus, I ask forgiveness for _____ [name any sin that comes to mind such as looking at porn, masturbation, lust, anger, unforgiveness, greed, or hate]."

- Pray the Lord's Prayer: "Our Father in heaven, hallowed be your name, your kingdom come, your will be done, on earth as it is in heaven. Give us today our daily bread, and forgive us our debts, as we also have forgiven our debtors. And lead us not into temptation, but deliver us from the evil one, for yours is the kingdom and the power and the glory forever. Amen" (Matthew 6:9-13).

- After praying the prayer, personalize it for your temptation. "Lord, please deliver me from the Tempter who is tempting me to _____. Lord, please deliver me from the Accuser who is telling me that my sin is not forgiven." If you are praying with a partner, the partner should say, "I agree in the name of Jesus."

Wounds and Triggers

- Ask the Holy Spirit to show you any wounds that are causing you to act out. Extend forgiveness to anyone who has hurt you. "Lord, I extend forgiveness to_____ for _____."

Amputate

- Separate yourself from any source of porn or lust-inducing environments. If you have just seen a pretty woman who is triggering you, begin to pray for her salvation, that she would find Christ and walk with Him.

Memorize Scripture

- Review your Scripture verses. Begin quoting out loud the verses from Psalm 103, Romans 6, EMAW verses, or any other memorized passages of Scripture.

Allies

- Call a brother for prayer when tempted, confess if you have blown it, and begin to go through these seven principles together.

Preach the Gospel to Yourself Daily

- "I thank You, Father, for the truth that 'there is now no condemnation for those who are in Christ Jesus' (Romans 8:1). I thank You, Jesus, for dying on the cross for me. I praise You that I am forgiven. You look at me as if I had never sinned, and I am adopted into Your family. You purchased me, and now I am free from sin."

WWW A MAP SEVEN KEYS TO FREEDOM

LESSON 7
Aggressive Worship Skill 3: Daily Offering and Armoring Our Bodies for Warfare

✓ Have the men break into pairs and recite all their *Every Man A Pure Warrior* verses to each other, and the hymn "Amazing Grace". If a man chose a different psalm, hymn, or spiritual song, have him quote the words to his partner. Have one person hold the cards and recite the hymn or song while the other checks for accuracy. Then have them switch roles.

✓ Count how many times you have practiced WWW A MAP in the last four weeks.

✓ Sign off on the *Completion Records*.

✓ Open the session with prayer.

✓ Go around the room, asking each man to share one Quiet Time.

✓ Begin reading the lesson paragraph by paragraph.

✓ Depending on time, have as many men as possible share their *Ask Questions*, meditations, and rewrites of Ephesians 6:11 and Romans 6:13.

✓ Read the *Points to Remember* and the *Assignment* for the next meeting.

✓ Break into pairs and practice WWW A MAP with each other. After one man works through it, have them reverse the roles.

WE MUST LEARN TO BE AGGRESSIVE WORSHIPERS OF THE LIVING GOD THROUGH THE DAILY OFFERING UP OF OUR BODIES AS AN ACT OF WORSHIP AND PUTTING ON THE ARMOR OF GOD AS AN ACT OF WARFARE.

GOD: WORTHY TO RECEIVE OFFERINGS

Ascribe to the LORD the glory due to his name; bring an offering and come into his courts. —PSALM 96:8

I had gone to the beach near my house for my daily Quiet Time. My times with the Lord had become a bit routine, they had become a drudgery. I'd gone through my mental checklist and was following the ABCs of a Quiet Time.

The passage I chose that day for my Quiet Time was Psalm 5. I cried out to God to speak to me, to reveal Himself to me. I asked Him to show me something new, something that would change me from the inside out. Here are the first three verses: *"Give ear to my words, O LORD; give heed to my groaning. Hearken to the sound of my cry, my King and my God, for to thee do I pray. O LORD, in the morning thou dost hear my voice; in the morning I prepare a sacrifice for thee, and watch"* (RSV).

As I mulled over this passage, it came to me that I should focus on verse 3. David said, *"In the morning I prepare a sacrifice for thee, and watch."* I asked myself, "What is my sacrifice? What could I bring to God that is something of worth?"

I remembered that many of the Old Testament priests offered daily animal sacrifices to God. Every week, Job offered sacrifices on behalf of his children. *"When a period of feasting had run its course, Job would make arrangements for them to be purified. Early in the morning he would sacrifice a burnt offering for each of them, thinking, 'Perhaps my children have sinned and cursed God in their hearts.' This was Job's regular custom"* (Job 1:5). I asked, "God, what sacrifice can I bring to You?"

As I pondered this, the Lord brought the following passages to mind. The first was Romans 12:1, followed by Romans 6:11-14, and then 1 Corinthians 6:18-20.

AGGRESSIVE WORSHIP SKILL 3: DAILY OFFERING AND ARMORING OUR BODIES FOR WARFARE

- ✓ Read or quote Romans 12:1, and note what God desires as an offering.

- ✓ Read Romans 6:11-14. What are the positive and negative commands listed here? What does it mean to "consider yourself dead?" Why does the Scripture mention offering *"every part of yourself"*? Read this passage in several different Bible translations to get the full meaning.

- ✓ Read 1 Corinthians 6:18-20. Who owns your body? What was the price paid for this ownership?

I had been struggling with the temptations of lust and sexual sin. As I wrestled with these temptations, I started listing the parts of my body and soul (mind, will, and emotions) that were involved in wrongdoing. As I recorded them, I started praying over every part of my being that was or is complicit in sin. The Holy Spirit was prompting me to specifically offer each part of my body and soul that He now owns back to Him as an offering. This was the answer to my question, "God, what sacrifice can I bring to You?" When I willfully and with full knowledge offer to God my body, my soul, and all my parts, I become the sacrifice that pleases Him. As I obey the promptings of the Holy Spirit in acts of obedience throughout the day, God is pleased with my practical, ongoing death to self and my being alive to Him.

✓ **Leaders**: Take some time as a group and have the men pray through some of the following suggested list of body parts. Pray about other body parts as they come to mind. Offer each body and soul part individually to God as an offering. I've written a sample prayer for the eyes.

Eyes: "Father, You made my eyes and have given me the ability to see. Thank You for the gift of sight. I give my eyes to You and dedicate them to You. Please turn my eyes from looking at vanities. Please put restraints and blinders on my eyes so that I might not look at anything that is defiling, base, or degrading. Please give me the desire to look upon You and to behold and see You and appreciate Your beauty."

Ears	**Sex organs/skin**
Desires/longings/appetites	**Hormones**
Mouth/tongue/lips	**Mind/will**
Heart/soul	**Emotions/fears/anxieties**

✓ Read Proverbs 7:6-23. Which body parts were involved to entice the young fool to sin?

As I thought about dedicating my whole body, body parts, and soul to God as an offering, God revealed that merely offering these parts was not enough. God wanted me to also *clothe* these body parts with His armor (Ephesians 6). As I dedicated my eyes, ears, tongue, mouth, brain, thoughts, emotions, fears, fantasies, dreams, and so on, He commanded me to put on the helmet of salvation, which covers all these parts of my being. As I dedicated my heart, emotions, desires, and vital organs to God, He also commanded me to put on the breastplate of righteousness.

I was meeting with a senior, enlisted army soldier who had been in several war zones, leading men in combat. Before each mission, one of his jobs was to inspect each member of his platoon to ensure that he was dressed correctly for battle. Every part of army-issued clothing and equipment was *required* to be worn in battle. In the same way, our Commander-in-Chief (God), commands us to wear specific pieces of clothing and armor when we engage the enemy. The act of putting on the armor is *not* optional from God's perspective. If we omit the step of putting on the spiritual armor that God commands us to use, we will fall prey to the schemes of the Enemy.

✓ Read Ephesians 6:10-18 and list the battle clothing that God commands us to wear every day.

✓ **Leaders**: Take some time as a group and have the men pray through the following list of armor that God commands us to put on. This exercise requires *faith*. To be frank, I don't fully understand how this works in the heavenlies. However, I do see visible results throughout the day when I am obedient to Him by intentionally offering my body and body parts to God and then putting on the armor over these same body parts that have been dedicated to Him. In the list, I've included samples of the things that I pray as I put on each piece of armor. Please use these as a guide. As you think and meditate on each piece, please pray using your own words, thoughts, and desires of your heart. These verses are from Ephesians 6 (RSV).

"Having girded your loins with truth" VERSE 14:
Father, by faith today I put on the belt of truth. Let all my actions and attitudes today be governed by truth, Your Word. I also want to be truthful in all that I say and do. I dedicate my sex organs to You, my hormones, my desires, and urges. Protect me and cover my loins with truth. Let me not be led astray by the deceitfulness of lust.

"Having put on the breastplate of righteousness" VERSE 14:
Father, by faith I put on the breastplate of righteousness. I praise You that You became sin for me so that I might become the righteousness of God. In Your strength, today help me do righteous things in righteous ways and with noble motives. Protect my heart and soul, all my emotions and feelings with the breastplate of righteousness.

"Having shod your feet with the equipment of the gospel of peace" VERSE 15:
> Father, by faith I put on my feet the equipment of the gospel of peace. Help me to be ready and prepared to share the gospel today with whomever you bring across my path. Help my eyes to see the lost and to lovingly engage them with the gospel. Lord, please bring people to me who are seeking You. Give me the boldness to engage and not shrink back in timidity when I have the opportunity to evangelize.

"Taking the shield of faith" VERSE 16:
> Father, by faith I take the shield of faith. Help me to trust You and to believe Your Word in all of my life choices today. Even when my senses tell me something contrary to Your Word, help me walk by faith and not by sight. Help me cling to Your promises, trusting in Your Word and Your character.

"Take the helmet of salvation and the sword of the Spirit, which is the word of God" VERSE 17:
> Father, by faith I put on the helmet of salvation. Father, please bring to remembrance all you have said to me (John 14:26). Help me to skillfully use your Word as I engage the enemy. Give me more of a hunger for You and Your Word (Psalm 119:20).

"Pray at all times in the Spirit, with all prayer and supplication" VERSE 18:
> Father, give me a spirit of prayer. Move me to pray more, more frequently, more fervently. Teach me how to become a man of prayer.

ASSIGNMENT 1: Memorize Ephesians 6:11.

Put on the full armor of God, so that you can take your stand against the devil's schemes. —EPHESIANS 6:11

✓ Meditate on Ephesians 6:11, using the *Ask Questions* method. Jot down two or three thoughts.

AGGRESSIVE WORSHIP SKILL 3: DAILY OFFERING AND ARMORING OUR BODIES FOR WARFARE

✓ Rewrite: Ephesians 6:11 in your own words. Be prepared to share this with the group.

ASSIGNMENT 2: Memorize Romans 6:13.

Do not offer any part of yourself to sin as an instrument of wickedness, but rather offer yourselves to God as those who have been brought from death to life; and offer every part of yourself to him as an instrument of righteousness.
—ROMANS 6:13

> **Ask Questions**
>
> **Is there:**
>
> A command to obey
>
> A promise to claim
>
> A sin to avoid
>
> An application to make
>
> Something new about God
>
> Ask: Who, What, When, Where, Why
>
> **Emphasize:**
> Different words
>
> **Rewrite**
> In your own words

✓ Meditate on Romans 6:13, using the *Ask Questions* method. Jot down two or three thoughts.

✓ Rewrite Romans 6:13 in your own words. Be prepared to share this with the group.

Points to Remember

1. The blood of Jesus bought us. He owns each part of our body.

2. When we offer ourselves back to God as a living sacrifice, that is our ultimate form of worship.

3. We are commanded to offer up not just our whole being, but each of our body parts (members) to God as a sacrifice.

4. God lays out spiritual clothing for us to wear every day.

5. By faith, in prayer, every day we are to put on each piece of clothing and armor to be prepared for spiritual warfare.

✓ To summarize this lesson, write out the most important things you learned.

✓ Record how many times you have practiced WWW A MAP over the last 4 weeks: _____

✓ **Leaders**: Have the men break into pairs and practice WWW A MAP with each other. Follow the model on pages 36–37. After one man works through it, have them reverse roles.

AGGRESSIVE WORSHIP SKILL 3: DAILY OFFERING AND ARMORING OUR BODIES FOR WARFARE

ASSIGNMENT FOR NEXT WEEK

1. Every day, get into the habit of offering your body and your body parts to God as a sacrifice. Start with your brain and work your way through your body, mentioning each part of your body that is used in sinning.

2. Every day, in faith and through prayer, put on each piece of God's armor.

3. Try to record five to seven Quiet Times this week from Ephesians 6:10-18 and Luke 10:1-20. It is okay to use one of your Quiet Times to complete the lesson and one to review portions of Psalm 103 and work on memorizing Romans 6:13 and Ephesians 6:11.

4. Practice worshiping God by singing hymns, songs, or psalms to God.

5. Place Ephesians 6:11 in the front window of your verse pack and memorize it this week. After memorizing it, then memorize Romans 6:13.

6. Finish any lessons that you have not completed.

7. Be prepared to share all your Every Man A Pure Warrior verses.

8. Read through and complete each question in the next lesson. Review and practice WWW A MAP every day, praying through each step.

WWW A MAP SEVEN KEYS TO FREEDOM

Worship

- Start worshiping God by praising Him. Sing your favorite hymn, psalm, or worship song. Offer your body and body parts to God as an act of worship and clothe your body with the armor of God.

Warfare Praying

- First, confess any known sin by praying and say the following spiritual warfare prayer. "Lord Jesus, I ask forgiveness for _____ [name any sin that comes to mind such as looking at porn, masturbation, lust, anger, unforgiveness, greed, or hate]."

- Pray the Lord's Prayer: "Our Father in heaven, hallowed be your name, your kingdom come, your will be done, on earth as it is in heaven. Give us today our daily bread, and forgive us our debts, as we also have forgiven our debtors. And lead us not into temptation, but deliver us from the evil one, for yours is the kingdom and the power and the glory forever. Amen" (Matthew 6:9-13).

- After praying the prayer, personalize it for your temptation. "Lord, please deliver me from the Tempter who is tempting me to _____. Lord, please deliver me from the Accuser who is telling me that my sin is not forgiven." If you are praying with a partner, the partner should say, "I agree in the name of Jesus."

Wounds and Triggers

- Ask the Holy Spirit to show you any wounds that are causing you to act out. Extend forgiveness to anyone who has hurt you. "Lord, I extend forgiveness to_____ for _____."

Amputate

- Separate yourself from any source of porn or lust-inducing environments. If you have just seen a pretty woman who is triggering you, begin to pray for her salvation, that she would find Christ and walk with Him.

Memorize Scripture

- Review your Scripture verses. Begin quoting out loud the verses from Psalm 103, Romans 6, EMAW verses, or any other memorized passages of Scripture.

Allies

- Call a brother for prayer when tempted, confess if you have blown it, and begin to go through these seven principles together.

Preach the Gospel to Yourself Daily

- "I thank You, Father, for the truth that 'there is now no condemnation for those who are in Christ Jesus' (Romans 8:1). I thank You, Jesus, for dying on the cross for me. I praise You that I am forgiven. You look at me as if I had never sinned, and I am adopted into Your family. You purchased me, and now I am free from sin."

LESSON 8
SPIRITUAL WARFARE 1: WAS I UNDER DEMONIC ATTACK?

✓ Have the men break into pairs and recite all their Every Man A Pure Warrior verses to each other beginning with Ephesians 6:11 and Romans 6:13. Have one man hold the cards and say the reference while the other man quotes the verse and says the reference at the end of the verse. Then have them switch roles.

✓ Sign off on the *Completion Records*.

✓ Open the session with prayer.

✓ Go around the room, asking each man to share one Quiet Time.

✓ Begin reading the lesson paragraph by paragraph.

✓ Depending on time, have as many men as possible share their *Ask Questions*, meditations and rewrites of 1 Peter 5:8 and the *Lord's Prayer*.

✓ Read the *Points to Remember* and the *Assignment*.

✓ Break into pairs and practice WWW A MAP with each other. After one man works through it, have them reverse the roles.

✓ This lesson is especially long and you may want to take two weeks on it. See break instruction on page 89.

WE MUST UNDERSTAND SPIRITUAL WARFARE AND LEARN HOW TO OVERCOME THE EVIL ONE. IF WE DON'T UNDERSTAND AND USE THIS KEY, WE WILL REMAIN LOCKED IN ENSLAVEMENT.

Was I Under Demonic Attack?

Satan is a formidable foe. His strategies to defeat us are many. He is a deceiver. He is a tempter. He is an accuser. He is a destroyer. He disguises himself as an angel of light. He is a slanderer. He can put thoughts into our heads. He has millions of demons under his command to harass, to afflict, and, if we allow them, to oppress us.

Bob's Story

Several years ago I was under attack again. The attack was oppressive. I found myself wanting to read the cheap, sensuous novels sold in grocery stores. I felt compelled to read these to stir up lust. Lust controlled me.

I felt defeated and again started thinking that 1 Corinthians 10:13 was just not true: *"No temptation has overtaken you except what is common to mankind. And God is faithful; he will not let you be tempted beyond what you can bear. But when you are tempted, he will also provide a way out so that you can endure it."*

I was staying in the basement at the home of a missionary, who had an extensive library. I walked up and down the rows of books and prayed, "God, I need help. Surely there is a book here that can help me. Please show me which book to read." Soon afterward several books on the topic of spiritual warfare caught my eye and I read them. Through these books, God answered my cries for help and expanded my understanding of Satan and spiritual warfare.

Before this time, I had never thought that there might be a demonic element to my struggle for purity. All these books spoke of my position in Christ and the power that we as believers possess because of Christ who lives in us. They offered various kinds of "warfare" prayers to pray. These were all new ideas for me. This lined up with Ephesians 6:18 (NIV) which tells us to pray *"on all occasions with all kinds of prayers and requests. With this in mind, be alert and always keep on praying for all the Lord's people."*

I followed the prompting of these books and, by praying, took authority over the demonic assaults. I prayed something like,

"Lord Jesus, thank You for Your death, burial, and resurrection on my behalf. I acknowledge Your lordship again over me and rejoice that I am part of Your family because of Your finished work on the cross. In Your name, Lord Jesus, I renounce all sinful activities connected with pornography and lust in my life. By the power of Your name and Your blood, I resist all demons of lust, pornography, impure thoughts, and immorality. Deliver me from the Evil One. Lead me not into temptation. Thank You, Lord, for Your mighty power and the authority You have given me as one of Your children."

Upon offering that prayer I felt an immediate release, akin to a physical weight lifting off my shoulders. I felt a freedom that I hadn't known for months. I was jubilant. I was discovering my spiritual authority in Christ! Praise God for the liberty only He can give us!

✓ What, if anything, stands out to you about spiritual warfare in Bob's story?

✓ If you have ever felt that you were possibly under a demonic attack, please describe that time.

✓ Lookup 1 John 2:12-14. What are the key growth markers mentioned that distinguish a young man from a spiritual child?

✓ In spiritual warfare ignorance only benefits the enemy. What does 2 Corinthians 2:11 teach will happen if we are unaware of how Satan works?

To successfully and consistently overcome the Evil One, we must know and understand basic facts about warfare.

1. We must know basic scriptural truths about our enemy Satan.

2. We must know his aims, purposes, and goals.

3. We must know the devil's tactics, how he operates, and when he plans to attack.

4. We must be able to recognize when we are under attack and realize how the Enemy lies.

It is not enough to simply know about Satan. To overcome his attacks in battle, we must know:

1. The power and authority of Jesus.

2. Our power, position, and authority as children of the living God.

3. How and when to skillfully use the weapons at our disposal.

4. How to identify and close any doors that we may have opened into our lives that give the devil a foothold to attack us.

The next several lessons will address many of these points.
1 John 2:12-14 speaks of the maturing process. I believe there are four district levels of awareness when it comes to spiritual warfare.

Level 1: A believer has a basic understanding of the spirit world, understands who Satan is, and what his goals are. The believer possesses a basic belief in the power of Jesus, that Jesus is the victor, and that greater is the Holy Spirit living within us than any demonic spirit sent to attack us. In the pursuit of sexual purity, a level 1 believer starts to connect the possibility that some of his purity struggles may be demonic oppression or temptation and not only his own natural, human, fleshly desires.

Level 2: A believer understands some of the spiritual weapons given to us so we can fight, and he is growing in the skill needed to use these weapons. A believer is growing in his ability to sense when he is about to be attacked and recognizes when he is under attack. And he is able to help other believers do the same. A believer has initial success in repelling and overcoming demonic attack.

Level 3: A believer continues to grow in the knowledge of Scripture, and understands the connection between wounds, family background, occult practices, and activities that open doors for demonic attack. He consistently sees victory over the Evil One and continues to grow in freedom from demonic oppression.

> **In spiritual warfare ignorance only benefits the enemy.**

Level 4: The believer has extensive experience in the use of spiritual weapons, and he adds regular fasting to his arsenal. He knows his position in Christ, and his spiritual senses have been trained. The believer is able to recognize demonic activity, has learned how to test the spirits, and through the power and authority of Jesus, intercedes for other demonized believers, freeing them from demonic oppression.

✓ Read the above four levels. What level are you currently? How important is it to you to grow in your understanding of spiritual warfare? Why?

Satan's Identity and Goals

✓ What names and purposes of Satan are revealed in the following verses?

Revelation 12:9-12

Matthew 4:1-3

Matthew 4:8-9

John 8:44

John 10:10

1 Peter 5:8-9

Job 1:6–2:10

Luke 22:31-32

✓ Write a paragraph about what you have learned from the above. Be prepared to share.

* Break here if you are spending two weeks on the lesson. If you are taking two weeks, have the men break into pairs and practice WWW A MAP.

How Often and When Does Satan Attack?

Scripture describes Satan as *"like a roaring lion looking for someone to devour"* (1 Peter 5:8). Satan is not playing games with us. He wants to discredit us. He wants to cause us misery. He hates our heavenly Father and all followers of Jesus. He wants to defeat us, devour us, and, if he could, destroy us. It is imperative that you become skillful at defeating this foe.

- ✓ Lookup Revelation 12:10. How often does Satan attack you, and by what method of attack?

Multiple times, every day, I wrestle with a "spiritual host of wickedness" (Ephesians 6:12 RSVCE). These attacks take the form of accusations, temptations, slander, and deceiving thoughts. John 13:2 says, *"The evening meal was in progress, and the devil had already prompted Judas, the son of Simon Iscariot, to betray Jesus."* Satan takes advantage of our natural tendencies to sin, reveals to us opportunities to rebel against God, and shows us how to disobey the Lord. Every believer should expect to be attacked every day with accusations, or slanders, or temptations or deceptive lies aimed at diminishing the greatness and goodness of God or their self-identity.

- ✓ Lookup Luke 4:13. When does Satan choose to attack us?

STABBS

The acrostic STABBS describes some of the opportune times when Satan attacks or shoots us with his flaming arrows.

Stressed: When we are under stress, we tend to want to escape. The porn industry offers us immediate stress release through lust and masturbation. When we are under pressure, we need to be on guard because we are vulnerable to attack.

Tired: General George Patton said, "Fatigue makes cowards out of us all." When we are tired mentally, physically, spiritually, and/or emotionally, Satan knows we are more vulnerable and may attack.

Alone: There is a reason Jesus sent his disciples out two by two. We were never meant to fight these battles alone. This is one of the reasons for marriage, "It is not good for man to be alone (Genesis 2:18)." I have seldom been tempted and acted on those temptations when I was with another like-minded Christian buddy or my wife.

Bored: Joe would fall after the week of finals, after all the tests were completed and all the projects had been submitted. He had time on his hands. When we are bored and not pressing toward a goal, we can quickly become distracted and assaulted by the Evil One.

Buzzed (alcohol, weed, high, etc.): Alcohol, pot, or other drugs lowers our inhibitions, making us vulnerable to demonic attack. Remember from Luke 4:13 (NET), after being commanded by Jesus to leave, that Satan left him, *"UNTIL A MORE OPPORTUNE TIME"* (emphasis mine). If you are buzzed, drunk, or high, you've opened the door to demonic attack.

Spiritual high: Less than twenty-four hours after calling down fire from heaven and killing the prophets of Baal, Elijah despaired for his very life. He was tired, lost perspective, and asked God to take him home. It was one of the spiritually highest points in the narrative of Israel. When we are on a spiritual high, we may be tempted to think that we have arrived or that sexual temptation is a thing of the past. First Corinthians 10:12 says *"So, if you think you are standing firm, be careful that you don't fall"* (NIV).

✓ Review the last two to three times you have fallen into porn, anger, or some other sin. Which of the above STABBS opportune times caused you to be vulnerable? Jot down two examples and be ready to share.

✓ When opportune times explained by STABBS are present in your life, what will you do to remain pure? Write down an application and be ready to share.

✓ **Leaders**: Have each man share when he is most vulnerable and his plan to combat the Enemy and win when he is attacked at an opportune time.

Warfare

Even though Satan is a defeated foe, he is still a formidable enemy. He has tremendous power.

When the children of Israel crossed the river Jordan into Canaan, God had promised to give them the land. But they still had to fight for it. As the Israelites fought, God pushed back their enemies and they possessed the land.

✓ According to Judges 3:1-2, what did God want his children and future generations to learn? See also Psalms 144:1.

✓ Read Ephesians 6:10-12 and 2 Corinthians 10:3-4. Write a paragraph titled "Why I Need to Be Prepared for Spiritual Warfare Battles?"

Four Admonitions in Scripture to Prepare for Battle

1. Jesus commanded in Matthew 26:41 *"Watch and pray that you may not enter into temptation; the spirit indeed is willing, but the flesh is weak"* (RSV). We are to continually be on guard, ever vigilant and watchful.

2. We are commanded to *"put on the full armor of God"* to be prepared for anticipated spiritual warfare (Ephesians 6:10-18). We are told to get dressed for battle.

3. We are told to be sober-minded and be watchful. *"Your adversary the devil prowls around like a roaring lion, seeking someone to devour"* 1 Peter 5:8 (ESV). We are told to not get drunk, lose our awareness, or dull our senses, but again, keep alert and watchful.

4. We are taught to pray in the Lord's Prayer, *"Lead us not into temptation, but deliver us from the evil one"* —Matthew 6:13. Here we are told to pray against Satan. This is the first prayer that we will use to develop our skills in defeating the Enemy.

✓ From the above admonitions how important is it for you to "prepare for battle?"

Using the Lord's Prayer to Resist Satan

Even with all these instructions and stories from Scripture, I never thought that my intense struggles in the pursuit of purity might have any connection at all with demonic activity.

When you sense that you are under attack, it is helpful to train yourself to immediately have a plan. Consider quoting out loud and praying the Lord's Prayer *and* calling your ally. Many of us who grew up in the church, have already memorized this great prayer. This is a basic, first step in learning how to fight. More advanced steps are in the lessons to follow.

I like to start with the Lord's Prayer and then, I personalize it, adding my own prayers and meditations. When praying through the prayer, I focus on *worshiping* God and on the spiritual *warfare aspects* of the prayer.

"Our Father in heaven, hallowed be your name, your kingdom come, your will be done, on earth as it is in heaven. Give us today our daily bread, and forgive us our debts, as we also have forgiven our debtors. **And lead us not into temptation, but deliver us from the evil one,** *for yours is the kingdom and the power and the glory forever. Amen (emphasis mine)"* —Matthew 6:9-13.

The following prayers from the Lord's Prayer are a type of daily warfare praying. These are examples of how to engage in spiritual warfare praying when we are tempted to sin or sense that we are under spiritual attack.

✓ **Leaders**: Have each man read one of the sentences from Matthew 6:9-13 and then the prayer example given.

"Our Father in heaven, hallowed be your name." The word hallowed simply means "holy." Other versions say, **"... may your name be kept holy"** (NLT) or **"... may your holy name be honored"** (GNT). —Matthew 6:9

> O Father, God, my God. You are holy; everything about You is holy. Your name is holy. Jesus died to take away my sin. Help me to love You. Help me to fight for holiness. Help me to honor Your Holy name by my choices and actions.

"Your kingdom come, your will be done, on earth as it is in heaven." —Matthew 6:10

> Father, You told me to seek first Your kingdom and Your righteousness (Matthew 6:33). Help me to obey this command. All of creation obeys You except the human heart. My heart wants to stray right now. Your will is for

me to love You, to obey You, to submit to You, and to follow You. Fulfill Your will in me. Live in me and empower me to do Your will (Psalm 143:10).

"Give us today our daily bread." —Matthew 6:11

Father, please continue to provide for me and my family. Not only our food, but also our emotional needs. Help me to receive from Your hand everything that I need for life and godliness (2 Peter 1:3-4). Give me also peace and freedom from fear, anxiety, lust, and anger. Give me the daily strength that I need to do Your will.

"And forgive us our debts, as we also have forgiven our debtors." —Matthew 6:12

Father, please forgive me for all my sins, particularly my sexual sin. Lord, every day, the Accuser reminds me of my sins. I've confessed these and You have forgiven me (1 John 1:9). Thank You for this forgiveness.

Lord, give me more grace to forgive those who have sinned against me and who have wounded me. Lord, by Your grace, I extend forgiveness to _____ [name those who have hurt you].

"And lead us not into temptation." —Matthew 6:13

Father, my flesh is so weak. Please lead me not into temptation or testing. Protect me from wrong thinking and the lies of the Enemy that would lead me to make bad decisions.

"But deliver us from the evil one." —Matthew 6:13

God, please deliver me. Put a shield around me and protect me from every attack from the Evil One. Give me the eyes to discern demonic attacks and understanding to recognize the schemes of Satan (2 Corinthians 2:11). Help me to resist the Enemy and take captive every thought raised against the knowledge of You (2 Corinthians 10:5). Help me to resist him and bring Scriptures to mind for me to quote and counter his lying words (John 14:26; James 4:7).

"For yours is the kingdom and the power and the glory forever. Amen."

—Matthew 6:13

SPIRITUAL WARFARE 1: WAS I UNDER DEMONIC ATTACK?

ASSIGNMENT 1: Memorize the Lord's Prayer. Matthew 6:9-13.

Our Father in heaven, hallowed be your name, your kingdom come, your will be done, on earth as it is in heaven. Give us today our daily bread. And forgive us our debts, as we also have forgiven our debtors. And lead us not into temptation, but deliver us from the evil one, for yours is the kingdom and the power and the glory forever. Amen.
—MATTHEW 6:9-13

✓ Rewrite the Lord's Prayer in your own words. Be prepared to share this with the group.

ASSIGNMENT 2: Memorize 1 Peter 5:8.

Be alert and of sober mind. Your enemy the devil prowls around like a roaring lion looking for someone to devour. —1 PETER 5:8

✓ Meditate on 1 Peter 5:8, using the *Ask Questions* method. Jot down two or three thoughts.

Ask Questions

Is there:

A command to obey

A promise to claim

A sin to avoid

An application to make

Something new about God

Ask: Who, What, When, Where, Why

Emphasize:
Different words

Rewrite
In your own words

✓ Rewrite 1 Peter 5:8 in your own words.

Points to Remember

1. We need to understand how often Satan attacks, how he attacks, how to recognize his attacks, and how to resist his attacks.

2. In spiritual warfare ignorance only benefits the enemy (2 Corinthians 2:11).

3. We need to identify times when we are especially vulnerable to Satan's attacks.

4. Jesus acknowledged spiritual warfare in the *Lord's Prayer* and gave us this prayer as one of our first weapons of warfare.

✓ Summarizing this lesson, write out your own most important things learned.

✓ Record how many times this week you practiced WWW A MAP: _____

✓ **Leaders**: Have the men break into pairs and practice WWW A MAP with each other. After one man works through it, have them reverse roles and have the other man work through it.

SPIRITUAL WARFARE 1: WAS I UNDER DEMONIC ATTACK?

ASSIGNMENT FOR NEXT WEEK

1. Record five to seven Quiet Times this week in the following passages: Revelation 12:7-12, Luke 4:1-13, Job 1–2, and 1 Peter 5:8.

2. Practice praying the *Lord's Prayer* every day as both an offensive and a defensive weapon.

3. Ask the Holy Spirit to alert your spirit this week to Satan's whispers. Ask the Lord to make you more spiritually alert when you are under attack.

4. Practice worshiping every day by quoting portions of Psalm 103. Practice every day the spiritual act of presenting your body and body parts to God as an offering, and practice putting on the armor of God.

5. Dedicate at least one day this week to worshiping God with songs, hymns, or spiritual songs.

6. Place the Lord's Prayer in the front window of your verse pack and memorize it this week. After mastering it, then put 1 Peter 5:8 in the window and memorize it.

7. Finish any lessons that you have not completed.

8. Be prepared to share all your Every Man A Pure Warrior verses.

9. Read and complete next week's lesson.

10. Practice WWW A MAP every day this week, focusing on spiritual warfare.

WWW A MAP — Seven Keys to Freedom

Worship
- Start worshiping God by praising Him. Sing your favorite hymn, psalm or worship song. Offer your body and body parts to God as an act of worship and clothe your body with the armor of God.

Warfare Praying
- First, confess any known sin by praying and say the following spiritual warfare prayer. "Lord Jesus, I ask forgiveness for _____ [name any sin that comes to mind such as looking at porn, masturbation, lust, anger, unforgiveness, greed, or hate]."
- Pray the Lord's Prayer: "Our Father in heaven, hallowed be your name, your kingdom come, your will be done, on earth as it is in heaven. Give us today our daily bread, and forgive us our debts, as we also have forgiven our debtors. And lead us not into temptation, but deliver us from the evil one, for yours is the kingdom and the power and the glory forever. Amen" (Matthew 6:9-13).
- After praying the prayer, personalize it for your temptation. "Lord, please deliver me from the Tempter who is tempting me to _____. Lord, please deliver me from the Accuser who is telling me that my sin is not forgiven." If you are praying with a partner, the partner should say, "I agree in the name of Jesus."

Wounds and Triggers
- Ask the Holy Spirit to show you any wounds that are causing you to act out. Extend forgiveness to anyone who has hurt you. "Lord, I extend forgiveness to _____ for _____."

Amputate
- Separate yourself from any source of porn or lust-inducing environments. If you have just seen a pretty woman who is triggering you, begin to pray for her salvation, that she would find Christ and walk with Him.

Memorize Scripture
- Review your Scripture verses. Begin quoting out loud the verses from Psalm 103, Romans 6, EMAW verses, or any other memorized passages of Scripture.

Allies
- Call a brother for prayer when tempted, confess if you have blown it, and begin to go through these seven principles together.

Preach the Gospel to Yourself Daily
- "I thank You, Father, for the truth that 'there is now no condemnation for those who are in Christ Jesus' (Romans 8:1). I thank You, Jesus, for dying on the cross for me. I praise You that I am forgiven. You look at me as if I had never sinned, and I am adopted into Your family. You purchased me, and now I am free from sin."

LESSON 9
SPIRITUAL WARFARE 2: THE JESUS WARFARE MODEL

✓ Have the men break into pairs and recite all their Every Man A Pure Warrior verses to each other, beginning with 1 Peter 5:8 and the Lord's Prayer. Have one man hold the cards and say the reference while the other man quotes the verse and says the reference at the end of the verse. Then have them switch roles.

✓ Sign off on the *Completion Records*.

✓ Open the session with prayer.

✓ Go around the room, asking each man to share one Quiet Time.

✓ Begin reading the lesson paragraph by paragraph.

✓ Depending on time, have as many men as possible share their *Ask Questions*, meditations, and rewrites of Luke 4:13 and 2 Corinthians 10:3-5.

✓ Read the *Points to Remember* and the *Assignment*.

✓ Break into pairs and practice WWW A MAP with each other. After one man works through it, have them reverse the roles.

This Lesson Explains More About How to Recognize and Understand Spiritual Warfare and How to Learn to Overcome the Evil One Using the Jesus Warfare Model.

The Jesus Warfare Model

Scripture records several conversations and interactions between Satan and humans. The first recorded dialogue is between Satan and Eve.

- ✓ Lookup Genesis 3:1-6 and focus on the conversation. Who initiated it? What questions were asked? What statements made? Did Eve know or realize that she was speaking with the Devil?

- ✓ Lookup John 13:1-8. Who put the thoughts in Judas's head? Do you think Judas had any clue that the urgings were from Satan? Was there any effort on Judas's part to resist?

In both of the above examples, I believe neither Eve nor Judas realized that Satan was in their presence. The ideas, thoughts, and questions came into their minds, but they never recognized satanic involvement.

✓ Lookup 2 Corinthians 10:5. What godly goal for our thought life do we find here?

One extended conversation that Jesus had with Satan is found in Luke 4:1-13 and Matthew 4:1-11. Jesus modeled for us both the awareness of recognizing Satan, and how to engage and fight the enemy.

✓ Lookup Luke 4:1-13 and Matthew 4:1-11. What do you observe about the method of fighting Satan? Who quoted Scripture in these passages and for what intent?

Paul warns us in 2 Corinthians 2:11 (RSV) that we must *"keep Satan from gaining the advantage over us; for we are not ignorant of his designs."* The challenge from 2 Corinthians 10:5 is to *"take captive every thought to make it obedient to Christ."* If we fail to do this and we believe any of the lying statements in the following section, we'll give in to sin, defeat, and despair. We must stand on the truth of God's Word, cling to Jesus, and believe while boldly resisting the Evil One.

The Jesus Warfare Model: Examples

The battles of accusation, temptation, slander, and condemnation begin when I wake up and before I am even out of my bed. Before I eat breakfast, many times I'm reminded of sin in general and usually some sexual sin that I committed. It's normally a sin that I have already confessed. The following are real-life, almost-every-day battles that I have with the Evil One. The method I use to daily fight the Accuser (Revelation 12:10), is the one Jesus used and modeled for us in defeating Satan, as found in Luke 4 and Matthew 4.

At some time during the day, almost *every day*, Satan reminds me of some sexual sin and says, "God hasn't forgiven you."

I reply, **"Begone, Satan, for it is written"** and I quote 1 John 1:9.

✓ Lookup and write down 1 John 1:9.

The Liar says, "Yeah, that's generally true, but God won't forgive that sin. It's too vile."

I reply, **"Begone, Satan, for it is written"** and I quote Psalm 103:2-3 or Colossians 2:11-15.

✓ Lookup Colossians 2:11-15 and Psalm 103:3. What truth in these two passages can help you defeat the above lie?

The slandering voice says, "You're a hypocrite, perverted, nasty, useless, unclean, and dirty."

I reply, **"Begone, Satan, for it is written"** and I quote John 15:3, 1 John 3:1, or 2 Timothy 2:21-22.

✓ Lookup these verses. How do these truths counter Satan's lies?

Satan continues, "Give up. Stop fighting. It will be easier for you to give in to lust than to waste all this energy fighting for purity."

I reply, **"Begone, Satan, for it is written"** and I quote Galatians 6:9 or Psalm 138:3.

✓ Lookup these two verses. How do they counter this lie?

The Accuser says, "You are guilty! You are condemned!"

I say, **"Begone, Satan, for it is written"** and I quote Romans 8:1-2.

✓ Lookup Romans 8:1-2. What does God say about condemnation in verse 1? What truth is found in verse 2?

The Deceiver says, "You can sin here. No one will know. No one will find out. You can do this and get away with it."

I say, **"Begone, Satan, for it is written"** and I quote Numbers 32:23.

✓ Try to summarize this verse in six words. Recite this verse when tempted.

>The Tempter says, "You would really enjoy sexual sin right now. You remember that was fun, wasn't it? Go ahead. It's not a sin to just look. As long as you don't touch."

I say, **"Begone, Satan, for it is written"** and I quote 2 Timothy 2:22 or Job 31:1.

> ✓ Lookup these two verses. Summarize the message they have for you.

>The Murderer says, "You can't live with the shame. You are better off dead than alive. Go ahead, stop the pain. Kill yourself."

I say, **"Begone, Satan, for it is written"** and I quote Galatians 2:20 or Romans 6:11.

> ✓ Lookup these verses. What truths counter the temptation to commit suicide?

This is spiritual warfare, like a firefight that goes on throughout the day, every day. When my mind is idle, the thoughts and suggestions come in. But to counter these, the Bible says we must *"take captive every thought to make it obedient to Christ"* (2 Corinthians 10:5). The methodology is to follow Christ's example. Satan attacks by suggestion and deception. Christ deflected the attacks by quoting Scripture.

> ✓ Which of these attacks have you experienced? How have you dealt with them?

✓ Are there other lies whispered to you that are *not* mentioned in the examples above? If so, write them here. What verses of truth would counter those lies?

ASSIGNMENT 1: Memorize Luke 4:13.

When the devil had finished all this tempting, he left him until an opportune time. —LUKE 4:13

✓ Meditate on Luke 4:13 using the *Ask Questions* method. Jot down two or three thoughts.

✓ Rewrite Luke 4:13 in your own words. Be prepared to share this with the group.

ASSIGNMENT 2: Memorize 2 Corinthians 10:3-5.

"For though we live in the world, we do not wage war as the world does. The weapons we fight with are not the weapons of the world. On the contrary, they have divine power to demolish strongholds. We demolish arguments and every pretension that sets itself up against the knowledge of God, and we take captive every thought to make it obedient to Christ." —2 CORINTHIANS 10:3-5

✓ Meditate on 2 Corinthians 10:3-5, using the *Ask Questions* method. Jot down some thoughts.

> **Ask Questions**
>
> **Is there:**
>
> A command to obey
>
> A promise to claim
>
> A sin to avoid
>
> An application to make
>
> Something new about God
>
> Ask: Who, What, When, Where, Why
>
> **Emphasize:**
> Different words
>
> **Rewrite**
> In your own words

✓ Rewrite 2 Corinthians 10:3-5 in your own words. Be prepared to share this with the group.

Last week we talked about different levels of spiritual warfare awareness. We started with using the Lord's Prayer as our first level of combat training response to the attacks of the Enemy. This lesson gave us additional combat training, using the Jesus Warfare Model.

Another level of combat training is exemplified in my opening story in lesson 8. It is a prayer based on our position in Christ and the power that we, as believers, have because of Christ's work on the cross. For me it was a turning point. I had struggled with porn, lust, shame and oppression. The prayer I prayed that night broke off the attack and began setting me free. It gave me the ability to begin to fight back against the Enemy's schemes, and I began to win and have freedom.

If you or someone you are ministering to is under significant attack from the enemy, PRAYING the following prayer has helped many people.

"Lord Jesus, thank You for Your death, burial, and resurrection on my behalf. I acknowledge Your lordship again over me and rejoice that I am part of Your family because of Your finished work on the cross. In Your name, Lord Jesus, I renounce all sinful activities connected with pornography and lust in my life. By the power of Your name and Your blood, I resist any and all demons of lust, pornography, impure thoughts, and immorality. Deliver me from the Evil One. Lead me not into temptation. Thank You, Lord, for Your mighty power and the authority You have given me as one of Your children."

Points to Remember

1. Satan has declared war on all believers. We should be watchful and expect daily assaults from the Evil One.

2. Jesus modeled how to repel the lies and suggestions of the Enemy. First, He recognized an attack from the Evil One. Then He commanded Satan to leave and quoted truth, a verse from Scripture, to counter the lie.

3. Satan hit Jesus with a barrage of lies, one after another. Jesus continued rebuking Satan and clung to and quoted Scriptural truth to defeat the Enemy.

4. Like Jesus we can say, "Begone Satan" and quote the Scripture.

✓ To summarize this lesson, write out the most important things you learned.

✓ **Leaders**: Have the men break into pairs and practice WWW A MAP with each other. After one man works through it, have them reverse roles.

✓ Record how many times this week you practiced WWW A MAP: _____

Assignment for Next Week

1. Try to record five to seven Quiet Times this week in the following passages: Ephesians 4:25-28; 2 Corinthians 2:5-11; Acts 5:1-10; 1 Samuel 15.

2. Dedicate at least one day this week to singing worship songs to God. If you know "A Mighty Fortress Is Our God," this hymn is perfect for this lesson.

3. Review Romans 6:13 and Psalm 103:8-12 every day. Learn them well; burn them into your brain. Every time you are tempted, quote one of these passages. Use Psalm 103 to worship God aggressively. On a daily basis, in prayer offer your body and body parts to God as an act of worship, and in faith pray and put on each piece of God's armor.

4. Continue to ask God to increase your spiritual awareness and to help you become more alert to demonic attack.

5. Place Luke 4:13 in the front window of your verse pack and memorize it this week. After you have memorized that verse, then place 2 Corinthians 10:3-5 in the verse pack window and memorize it.

6. Finish any lessons not completed. Read the next lesson, answering all the questions.

7. Be prepared to share all your Every Man A Pure Warrior verses.

8. Practice WWW A MAP every day this week, focusing again on spiritual warfare.

Worship

- Start worshiping God by praising Him. Sing your favorite hymn, psalm, or worship song. Offer your body and body parts to God as an act of worship and clothe your body with the armor of God.

Warfare Praying

- First, confess any known sin by praying and say the following spiritual warfare prayer. "Lord Jesus, I ask forgiveness for _____ [name any sin that comes to mind such as looking at porn, masturbation, lust, anger, unforgiveness, greed, or hate]."

- Pray the Lord's Prayer: "Our Father in heaven, hallowed be your name, your kingdom come, your will be done, on earth as it is in heaven. Give us today our daily bread, and forgive us our debts, as we also have forgiven our debtors. And lead us not into temptation, but deliver us from the evil one, for yours is the kingdom and the power and the glory forever. Amen" (Matthew 6:9-13).

- After praying the prayer, personalize it for your temptation. "Lord, please deliver me from the Tempter who is tempting me to _____. Lord, please deliver me from the Accuser who is telling me that my sin is not forgiven." If you are praying with a partner, the partner should say, "I agree in the name of Jesus."

Wounds and Triggers

- Ask the Holy Spirit to show you any wounds that are causing you to act out. Extend forgiveness to anyone who has hurt you. "Lord, I extend forgiveness to_____ for _____."

Amputate

- Separate yourself from any source of porn or lust-inducing environments. If you have just seen a pretty woman who is triggering you, begin to pray for her salvation, that she would find Christ and walk with Him.

Memorize Scripture

- Review your Scripture verses. Begin quoting out loud the verses from Psalm 103, Romans 6, EMAW verses, or any other memorized passages of Scripture.

Allies

- Call a brother for prayer when tempted, confess if you have blown it, and begin to go through these seven principles together.

Preach the Gospel to Yourself Daily

- "I thank You, Father, for the truth that 'there is now no condemnation for those who are in Christ Jesus' (Romans 8:1). I thank You, Jesus, for dying on the cross for me. I praise You that I am forgiven. You look at me as if I had never sinned, and I am adopted into Your family. You purchased me, and now I am free from sin."

LESSON 10
SPIRITUAL WARFARE 3: STEPS TO RESIST DEMONIC OPPRESSION

✓ Have the men break into pairs and recite all their *Every Man A Pure Warrior* verses to each other, beginning with 2 Corinthians 10:3-5, Luke 4:13 and 1 Peter 5:8. Have one man hold the cards and say the reference while the other man quotes the verse and says the reference at the end of the verse. Then have them switch roles.

✓ Sign off on the *Completion Records*.

✓ Open the session with prayer.

✓ Go around the room, asking each man to share one Quiet Time.

✓ Begin reading the lesson paragraph by paragraph.

✓ Depending on time, have as many men as possible share their *Ask Questions*, meditations, and rewrites of James 4:7, 2 Corinthians 2:11, and Ephesians 4:26-27.

✓ Read the *Points to Remember* and the *Assignment*.

✓ Break into pairs and practice WWW A MAP with each other. After one man works through it, have them reverse the roles.

This Lesson Explains More About How to Recognize and Understand Spiritual Warfare and How to Learn to Overcome the Evil One.

Eli's Story

Eli's folks divorced, and his father remarried when Eli was fourteen years old; he then lived with his younger stepsister. They all went to church regularly, and the whole family accepted Jesus and started to follow the Lord.

When Eli was sixteen, hormones had kicked in for both him and his stepsister. There was sexual tension between them, and eventually, they both gave in and had sex. But his stepsister was only fifteen. Guilt and shame immediately consumed them both. They confessed it to God, their youth pastor, and their parents and sought forgiveness from them and each other.

When Eli turned eighteen, partly out of shame and embarrassment, and to escape the ongoing sexual tension, he left home and joined the military. As he reflected on his life, a thought occurred to him: *I had sex with a minor.* The more he dwelt on this sin, the more shameful he felt. Then another thought came to his mind: *You're a pedophile.* And that thought sank into his heart and soul and changed how he saw himself.

Now, since he self-identified as a pedophile, he took the precaution of avoiding anyone who was a minor. He walked around with a cloud of darkness over him. He felt no joy. He had a sense of desperation about him, and he was in agony. When he was thirty-three years old, he asked me, "Can you help me?"

In Matthew 12:43-45, Jesus illustrates a vital principle of spiritual warfare. He said that when a man is delivered from a demon, the demon roams about the earth, looking for a new home. Unable to find one, he goes back to his original home, and if he sees it empty, swept, and in good order, he finds seven more demons even more evil than himself and brings them back to live with him in that home. An application of this story is that this man's house was empty, not filled. We need to fill "our house" with the indwelling of the Spirit of Jesus Christ through ongoing worship, Scripture memory, meditation, singing, and so on.

As believers, we are bought and paid for by Jesus through His paying the redemption price for our sins. When we repent and invite Jesus to dwell in our hearts, He makes us alive and comes to live inside us, uniting with our newly quickened spirit. He owns us.

Giving Opportunity to Satan; Open Doors

But being a believer does not free us from possible oppression. Paul warns us in Ephesians 4:26-27, *"'In your anger do not sin.' Do not let the sun go down while you are still angry, and do not give the devil a foothold."* Unresolved anger or other sins we hold on to can give the devil a foothold. Unwittingly, even as believers, we can open doors that invite demons to attack us. The Greek word for foothold means opportunity or place. We are not to give any room, place or opportunity for the Evil One to gain a foothold in our lives or thinking.

In 2 Corinthians 2:11, God calls us to forgive *"in order that Satan might not outwit us."* We are commanded to forgive as the Lord forgave us. When we are hurt and choose not to forgive, but instead hold a grudge, we give demons an open door.

Another open door is when we indulge the flesh by looking at pornography and/or let our minds wander into sexual fantasies. Romans 13:14 says, *"Rather, clothe yourselves with the Lord Jesus Christ, and do not think about how to gratify the desires of the flesh."* Heed this verse or you give impurity room to reign in your thinking.

A third open door is the occult. Deuteronomy 18:10-12 (ESV) warns us *"There shall not be found among you anyone who burns his son or his daughter as an offering, anyone who practices divination or tells fortunes or interprets omens, or a sorcerer or a charmer or a medium or a necromancer or one who inquires of the dead, for* **whoever does these things is an abomination to the Lord** (emphasis mine)." If we engage with the occult by visiting fortune-tellers, playing with an Ouija board, visiting palm readers, going to séances, trying to contact the dead, seeking a reading from tarot cards, or otherwise involving ourselves with the occult, we open the door to demonic attack and oppression.

> ✓ Spend some time praying about anger, unforgiveness, indulging the flesh, and engaging with the occult. Ask the Lord to bring to mind

ways you may have given the Enemy an opportunity to attack you, or how you have given the devil a foothold. List these things below and we will pray through them in step 4 of the next section.

The Bible gives us many practical steps for any believer to escape demonic oppression. The basis of all deliverance is the completed, victorious work of Christ on the cross. The life and sacrificial death of Jesus give us this foundation for freedom.

Because of the power given to us as followers of Jesus (Acts 1:8), and because of our new position being seated with Christ in the heavenlies, when we recognize that we are under demonic attack, we will have the power to resist (Ephesians 6:13, James 4:7, and 1 Peter 5:9).

Many of the following steps will help you to recognize when Satan is at your door, and how to close any open doors that you may have opened to Satan. They may have been opened because of your former life before becoming a believer. Or, perhaps some of your family members were involved in the occult. Or, you made foolish choices by making vows, or joining Satanic organizations, and thereby giving ground to Satan.

STEPS TO RESIST SATAN AND DEMONIC OPPRESSION

1. Speak your testimony. In Revelation 12:11, we are told that believers overcome Satan by *"the word of their testimony."* Open your time of prayer by verbalizing your testimony of following Jesus. You can pray like this:

> *"Father, I come to You in the name of the Lord Jesus. Thank You, Jesus, for dying on the cross for me. I affirm afresh that I believe in You. I believe that Your sacrifice paid the price due because of my multitudes of sin. I believe that Your blood redeemed me and forgives my sin and that You have justified me and sanctified me and that Your blood continuously cleanses me"* (See Ephesians 1:7 and 1 John 1:7).

2. Humble yourself. We know from 1 Peter 5:5-6 that God opposes the proud but gives grace to the humble. We also know from John 15:5 that apart from Jesus we can do nothing. Continue your time of prayer like this:

> "Lord Jesus, I glory in You. I affirm that apart from You I am nothing and can do nothing. I affirm that everything I have that is good has come as a gift from Your generous hand. I affirm that You are all and everything, and I humble myself before You."

3. Confess. Psalm 32:3-5 says, *"When I kept silent, my bones wasted away through my groaning all day long. For day and night your hand was heavy on me; my strength was sapped as in the heat of summer. Then I acknowledged my sin to you and did not cover up my iniquity. I said, 'I will confess my transgressions to the Lord.' And you forgave the guilt of my sin."*

Continue in prayer, confessing any sins that you are aware of.

4. Repent. After confessing your sins, verbally renounce and repent of those sins. Titus 2:11-12 says *"For the grace of God has appeared that offers salvation to all people. It teaches us to say 'No' to ungodliness and worldly passions, and to live self-controlled, upright and godly lives in this present age."* Review the things you listed above and continue your prayer like this:

> "Father, I repent of the sins of _____. I renounce _____. Please give me the strength to depend on You and to remove any provisions that I have made to continue in that sin."

5. Forgive. This is the time to extend forgiveness to anyone who has wronged you or sinned against you as Ephesians 4:32 says, *"Be kind to one another, tenderhearted, forgiving one another, as God in Christ forgave you"* (ESV). Forgiveness is an act of obedience and the will, not emotions. We must obey God whether we feel like it or not. Obedience is always an act of the will. Continue praying like this:

> "Father, I come now and lay down my right to be angry at_____. They hurt and wounded me, but I am reminded and am aware that I have wounded and hurt You by my rebellion and disobedience. Yet You still forgive me. Father, by Your grace I forgive _____ and cancel any debt that I feel they owe me. Please bless them with knowledge of You. Fill me with the same love for them as You have for me."

6. Renounce and repent of any involvement with the occult. This includes any cultic activities that you or your family, or your ancestors have committed. This follows the example found in Acts 19:18-19 (ESV) *"Many also of those who were now believers came, confessing and divulging their practices. And a number of those who practiced magic arts brought their books together and burned them in the sight of all."* It also follows the example of Nehemiah 9:2 (ESV) *"And the Israelites separated themselves from all foreigners and stood and confessed their sins and the iniquities of their fathers."* Pray like this:

> "Father, in the name of Jesus and by faith I renounce and repent of any and all involvement that I have had with the occult, and I repent of all cultic involvement that my family has had. Please forgive me when I practiced cultic activities."

7. Curses. Many in the occult curse followers of Jesus. If you sense evil supernatural forces arrayed against you, your family, or your ministry, then follow the teachings of Romans 12:14 and *"Bless those who persecute you; bless and do not curse them"* (ESV). Pray like this:

> "Father, in the name of Jesus, I bless those who are cursing me. I pray that You would convict them of sin, righteousness and judgment, that their eyes would be opened, and that You would draw them to a saving knowledge of Jesus. Bless them in the name of Jesus."

8. Renounce and repent of family sins. The Scriptures say that the sins of the father are passed down to the second, third, and fourth generations. Many times, we know the sins or character traits of family members. My family has a history of adultery. My wife's family is known for their anger, bitterness, and grudges. Pray like this:

> "Lord Jesus, I renounce and repent of the sins of my father and mother, grandfathers and grandmothers, and great-grandfathers and great-grandmothers, specifically the sins of _____. In Your name and through Your grace, please give me the strength to overcome the tendency to sin in the same way."

9. Renounce and repent of vows and oaths. Another opportunity for evil is opened by vows and oaths that we make. When we say, "I will never ...," that becomes a vow. Vows made in anger or haste, when someone has wounded or offended us, invite evil into our lives. Jesus said in Matthew 5:34 *"But I tell you, do not swear an oath at all."* Almost always, we end up becoming or doing what we swore that we would never be or do. Another open door for demons is swearing allegiance to some type of organization, club, or order. If applicable, pray something like this:

> "Father, I renounce and repent of the vow or oath I made to join _____. Please forgive me. I take back the ground that I yielded to the Evil One by making that vow or oath."

10. Submit to God. James 4:7 says we are to submit to God before we resist the devil. This is another act of our declaration of dependence on God. Pray like this:

> "Father, I submit to You and to Your authority. I yield myself and all my rights to You. Thank You for adopting me and raising me up with You to be seated with You in the heavenlies."

11. Resist or expel any demons. Because we are seated with Christ, are justified, redeemed, and sanctified, and have received power from Jesus, and because *"the one who is in you is greater than the one who is in the world"* (1 John 4:4), we can resist demons and overcome their influence. Pray like this:

> "Father, in the name of Jesus and because of the power of the Holy Spirit in me, I resist demonic influences in my life, specifically _____ and _____." Name whatever it is that you are consistently struggling with. That could be depression, confusion, fear, anxiety, lust, same-sex attraction, evil desires, compulsiveness, impurity, hatred, anger, rage, bitterness, sloth, suicidal thoughts, or something else.

12. Praise and Repeat. You may not feel anything, but you have just exerted tremendous spiritual power in the heavenlies. Enter into a time of praise. This is not a "one and done" process. As you continue in ministry and growth, you will come under more and varied forms of attack. Repeat this process as often as you feel it is needed. [5]

> ✓ **Leaders:** Have the men break into pairs and pray through the model prayers in the twelve practical steps of resisting Satan.

Returning to the story of Eli, who had sex with his stepsister and then felt that he was a pedophile: a pack of demons was afflicting him. First, *a spirit of deception* was on him. He was sixteen, and she was fifteen when

---

[5] These twelve steps adapted from Derek Prince, *They Shall Expel Demons: What You Need to Know About Demons—Your Invisible Enemies* (Bloomington, Minnesota, Chosen Books, 1998).

they had sex. That hardly makes him a pedophile. Legally and technically, he was still a minor.

There was also a *spirit of accusation* resting on him. Revelation 12:10 says that Satan accuses us night and day. When the thought came to Eli that he was a pedophile, *an accusing, lying spirit of slander* was seeking to afflict him. For more than fifteen years, every day, he heard the same condemning accusation: "You're a pedophile, you're a pedophile."

A spirit of *shame and condemnation* was resting on him. All these spirits were acting like a thief to rob him of joy. He had repented, had sought forgiveness, and had been forgiven by his parents and his stepsister, but Satan is a master at making us carry the guilt of already-confessed sin. Since Eli was still struggling with lust and impure thoughts, *a spirit of lust* and *a spirit of incest*, still resided in him. These spirits needed to be called out and expelled.

I led Eli through all twelve steps of escaping demonic oppression. He professed his testimony and love for Jesus. He declared his humility before God. He confessed and repented of all sins that the Holy Spirit brought to mind. He renounced and confessed all sins of his ancestors, all oaths and vows, and any and all involvement with the occult. Then he prayed a personalized version of the Lord's Prayer. After which I said, "I agree in the name of Jesus." And Eli immediately felt a lifting of heaviness. After completing this process, we entered into a time of praise and worship.

Repeat this process as needed. This made a huge difference for Eli and for dozens of other men I have counseled. There may be multiple layers of wounds and hurts, things buried in your life, each one requiring cleansing. If you sense there is a demonic presence, take authority and go through these twelve steps.

For more advanced warfare prayer instruction, please see "Biblical Foundations" in the Appendix.

ASSIGNMENT 1: Memorize James 4:7.

Submit yourselves, then, to God. Resist the devil, and he will flee from you.   —JAMES 4:7

- ✓ Meditate on James 4:7, using the *Ask Questions* method. Jot down two or three thoughts.

- ✓ Rewrite James 4:7 in your own words. Be prepared to share this with the group.

ASSIGNMENT 2: Memorize Ephesians 4:26-27.

In your anger do not sin. Do not let the sun go down while you are still angry, and do not give the devil a foothold. —EPHESIANS 4:26-27

- ✓ Meditate on Ephesians 4:26-27, using the *Ask Questions* method. Jot down two or three thoughts.

- ✓ Rewrite Ephesians 4:26-27 in your own words. Be prepared to share this with the group.

Assignment 3: Memorize 2 Corinthians 2:11.

... in order that Satan might not outwit us. For we are not unaware of his schemes. —2 Corinthians 2:11

✓ Meditate on 2 Corinthians 2:11 using the *Ask Questions* method. Jot down two or three thoughts.

> **Ask Questions**
>
> **Is there:**
>
> A command to obey
>
> A promise to claim
>
> A sin to avoid
>
> An application to make
>
> Something new about God
>
> Ask: Who, What, When, Where, Why
>
> **Emphasize:**
> Different words
>
> **Rewrite**
> In your own words

✓ Rewrite 2 Corinthians 2:11 in your own words. Be prepared to share this with the group.

✓ **Leaders**: Have the men break into pairs and practice WWW A MAP with each other. After one man works through it, have them reverse roles.

✓ Record how many times this week you practiced WWW A MAP: _____

Points to Remember

1. Anger, unforgiveness, indulging in the flesh, and engaging in the occult are all open doors that allow Satan to get a foothold in our lives.

2. When we confess our sin, forgive others, renounce any involvement with the occult, bless those who curse us, and so on, we shut the doors that we have opened that allow demons to attack us.

3. Satan will flee from us when we draw near to God and resist the Devil.

✓ To summarize this lesson, write out the most important things you learned.

EVERY MAN A WARRIOR

ASSIGNMENT FOR NEXT WEEK

1. Try to record five to seven Quiet Times this week in the following passages: Psalm 73, Isaiah 52:13-15, and Isaiah 53.

2. Dedicate at least one day this week to singing worship songs to God. If you know "A Mighty Fortress Is Our God," this hymn is perfect for this lesson.

3. Review Romans 6:13 and Psalm 103:8-12 every day. Learn them well; burn them into your brain. Every time you are tempted, quote one of these passages. Use Psalm 103 to worship God aggressively. Daily, in prayer offer your body and body parts to God as an act of worship, and in faith pray and put on each piece of God's armor.

4. Continue to ask God to increase your spiritual awareness and to help you become more alert to demonic attacks.

5. Place James 4:7 in the front window of your verse pack and memorize it this week. After you have memorized that verse, then place Ephesians 4:26-27 followed by 2 Corinthians 2:11 in the verse pack window and memorize them.

6. Finish any lessons not completed. Read the next lesson, answering all the questions.

7. Be prepared to share all your Every Man A Pure Warrior verses.

8. Practice WWW A MAP every day this week, focusing again on spiritual warfare.

WWW A MAP — SEVEN KEYS TO FREEDOM

Worship

- Start worshiping God by praising Him. Sing your favorite hymn, psalm, or worship song. Offer your body and body parts to God as an act of worship and clothe your body with the armor of God.

Warfare Praying

- First, confess any known sin by praying and say the following spiritual warfare prayer. "Lord Jesus, I ask forgiveness for _____ [name any sin that comes to mind such as looking at porn, masturbation, lust, anger, unforgiveness, greed, or hate]."

- Pray the Lord's Prayer: "Our Father in heaven, hallowed be your name, your kingdom come, your will be done, on earth as it is in heaven. Give us today our daily bread, and forgive us our debts, as we also have forgiven our debtors. And lead us not into temptation, but deliver us from the evil one, for yours is the kingdom and the power and the glory forever. Amen" (Matthew 6:9-13).

- After praying the prayer, personalize it for your temptation. "Lord, please deliver me from the Tempter who is tempting me to _____. Lord, please deliver me from the Accuser who is telling me that my sin is not forgiven." If you are praying with a partner, the partner should say, "I agree in the name of Jesus."

Wounds and Triggers

- Ask the Holy Spirit to show you any wounds that are causing you to act out. Extend forgiveness to anyone who has hurt you. "Lord, I extend forgiveness to_____ for _____."

Amputate

- Separate yourself from any source of porn or lust-inducing environments. If you have just seen a pretty woman who is triggering you, begin to pray for her salvation, that she would find Christ and walk with Him.

Memorize Scripture

- Review your Scripture verses. Begin quoting out loud the verses from Psalm 103, Romans 6, EMAW verses, or any other memorized passages of Scripture.

Allies

- Call a brother for prayer when tempted, confess if you have blown it, and begin to go through these seven principles together.

Preach the Gospel to Yourself Daily

- "I thank You, Father, for the truth that 'there is now no condemnation for those who are in Christ Jesus' (Romans 8:1). I thank You, Jesus, for dying on the cross for me. I praise You that I am forgiven. You look at me as if I had never sinned, and I am adopted into Your family. You purchased me, and now I am free from sin."

LESSON 11
WOUNDS 1: PORN IS MEETING A NEED IN YOUR LIFE

✓ Have the men break into pairs and recite James 4:7; 2 Corinthians 2:11, and Ephesians 4:26,27 to each other.

✓ Count how many times you have practiced WWW A MAP in the last four weeks.

✓ Sign off on the *Completion Records*.

✓ Open the session with prayer.

✓ Go around the room, asking each man to share one Quiet Time.

✓ Begin reading the lesson paragraph by paragraph.

✓ Depending on time, have as many men as possible share their *Ask Questions*, meditation, and rewrites of Psalm 62:8.

✓ Read the *Points to Remember* and the *Assignment*.

✓ Break into pairs and practice WWW A MAP with each other. After one man works through it, have them reverse the roles.

This is the First of Three Lessons That Will Discuss the Impact of Wounds and Trauma on Purity Struggles Later in Life.

My Battle for Purity

In my battle for purity, I was caught in cycles of sin that left me hopeless, discouraged, and depressed. Unfortunately, habit patterns that develop in young men never stop, unless these habits are identified, purposefully challenged, and aggressively changed for years.

After I became a believer, my infatuation with porn continued. Porn became my mistress and my lover. Even after finding out that I was not alone, I still struggled with lust, porn, and masturbation. Even after getting married and fathering children, leaving my career, and going into full-time vocational Christian ministry, I slipped back into my childhood practice. I knew it was wrong, could quote verses to anyone about God's perspective on the topic, yet still could not figure out why porn had such allure and such a hold on me.

Several years after I joined the ministry, an older, godly disciplemaker came for a visit. He asked me if there was an area in my life that I needed or wanted to change. I very cautiously told him, "I want to know why I keep wanting to look at porn. I know it's wrong, but I still desire it in my heart of hearts. And I want to know why I can't cry."

He started asking me questions about my life and childhood. I could not recall anything before ten years of age. As he probed deeper, I could not remember anything before the night my dad left our family.

He gave me the assignment of reconstructing that horrible night. My mother and three older brothers and sisters were available, and I interviewed them all. It did not make a pretty picture.

My mom was on the floor, literally holding on to my dad's leg, trying to prevent him from leaving. My mom's sister was in the corner laughing a strange laugh. "Let him go, Avon, he's no good for you." My mom was crying, my aunt was laughing, and my dad was screaming at all five of us children to get back into our bedrooms and shut our doors.

When my dad finally walked out the front door. I was a tearful wreck. According to my family, I cried nonstop for three days. My crying bugged my brothers and sisters, and they reported this to my dad when he showed up.

He pulled me aside and asked me, "Do you want to be a man when you grow up?" Through tears, I sobbed, "Yes." Then he said, "Then you need to stop crying. Real men don't cry. Will you promise me that you will stop crying?" I tearfully nodded my head and said, "I promise." I immediately stopped crying and have mostly had dry eyes ever since.

After I made that vow to my father, many lies were planted, such as "Emotions are bad; don't feel" and "Men don't cry; you're not a real man if you show emotions." These lies became strongholds in my life that still afflict me to this day.

I told the old disciplemaker my story. Before he left, he gave me one more assignment. "The next time you find yourself looking for porn, ask the Holy Spirit to stop you and ask Him, *'What need am I seeking to meet through porn right now?'*"

> **We worship our way into an addiction by continually yielding in our hearts to whatever gives us refuge, reward, comfort, and so forth. It could be alcohol, drugs, or video games. But in our culture, *porn* and *sexual sin* have risen to the number one form of worship. To escape this, we must worship our way out of enslavement by focusing our time, energy, money, and hearts to the pursuit of and the glorifying of God.**

I gave him a funny look. He said, "You think this is nonsense, don't you?" I nodded. He confidently said, "You will look for porn again. Porn is meeting a need in your life. That's why it has such a stranglehold on you." I dismissively said, "I am just a lustful guy, and porn just helps me fulfill my desires." He countered that by saying, "As a little boy, your dad's leaving you crushed you. You were deeply wounded, and in your hurt, you were looking for comfort, someone, or something to deaden the pain of your broken heart. When you were offered porn, you found a quick fix, something to deaden the hurt, a salve to put on your wound."

He repeated his assignment, "You'll look for porn again, and when you do, ask the Holy Spirit to reveal to you what is happening in your soul." I nodded and said, "I'll try it."

I had never connected my childhood trauma—an absentee dad, divorce, and abandonment—with my ongoing struggles for purity. I had always dismissed such thoughts as foolishness. What the wise, older disciplemaker was saying is illustrated in the following diagram.

The Sexual Sin Cycle

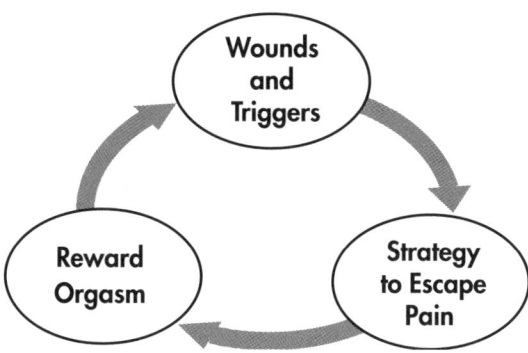

Sure enough, two weeks later I was out cruising for porn. I had stopped in front of a bookstore where I knew I could find lust-inducing stuff, and the Holy Spirit reminded me of the previous conversation. So I asked Him, "Why am I seeking porn right now?" I did not expect a response, so I was surprised when the Holy Spirit said to me, "You are anxious."

I replied, "About what?" He said, "Money." He was right. The total income we missionaries received was whatever people donated to keep us on the mission field. I agreed with the Spirit and then said, "I *am* anxious about money. Are you going to provide for us?"

Immediately the Holy Spirit brought Philippians 4:19 to mind: *"... my God will meet all your needs."* I nodded and thanked Him for this promise from the Word. Then I asked, "What am I supposed to do about this anxiety?" He immediately brought another verse to mind that I had memorized, 1 Peter 5:7: *"Cast all your anxiety on him because he cares for you."* Then I said, "What? You want me to tell you my feelings?" I felt both stupid and uncomfortable. I never told anyone about my feelings. I had been taught that it was unmanly to talk about feelings. I continually buried them. Now the Holy Spirit was asking me to talk to Him about my innermost hurts, fears, and wounds.

I then asked the Lord, "What does all this have to do with porn?" Once more, the Spirit reminded me of the conversation with the disciplemaker. The wise, older man had said, "Porn is meeting a need in your life." I again asked the Spirit what need was being met, and He brought another verse to mind, Psalm 62:8: *"Trust in him at all times, you people; pour out your hearts to him, for God is our refuge."* He then whispered to my soul, "You are seeking refuge to escape the pain of anxiety. You don't want to feel any negative emotions. You seek to deaden your pain with porn. You are making porn your refuge, your safe place." God was saying, "I want to be your refuge and reward. I want to be that safe place for you."

Not only was I finding temporary emotional escape in porn, but I was being rewarded by the pursuit of porn and by acting out through masturbation.

The Spirit went on to say, "Porn is an idol for you. When you seek to get needs met apart from Me—the very needs that I have promised to meet—you are substituting porn for Me. This makes you an idolater. You are worshiping porn instead of Me.

- ✓ Review Bob's story pages 124-127. What are your thoughts? Jot down at least three observations.

- ✓ Do you believe there is a connection between childhood wounds and the escape through porn? Why or why not?

- ✓ Are there any wounds in your life that you have sought to deaden or escape from through the pursuit of porn and lust? Ask the Holy Spirit to bring to mind anything He wants to reveal. Be prepared to share with your group.

✓ Look at the following verses and note any truths about finding refuge in God.

Psalm 46:1

Psalm 62:5-8

✓ Write a short paragraph, based on these verses, about what it means to make God your refuge.

There are many different ways to deal with emotions. King David reveals to us a good way to handle them. He expressed them to God. David poured out his heart to God regularly. He was a poet and a songwriter. He would tell God his ups and downs, pouring out his anger and his frustration, and asking God to smash his enemies. He even asked God, *"... where is your steadfast love ..."* Psalm 89:49 (ESV) and *"How long, O Lord? Will you be angry forever?"* (Psalm 79:5). God's door is always open. He is *delighted* when we pour out our hearts and souls to Him. He can handle all of our emotions, no matter how dark and ugly they are.

Unfortunately for me, my father crushed my ability to cry or handle my emotions. I was not taught how to deal with hurtful, negative emotions. I was taught that it was shameful to cry and unmanly to express feelings.

Right after my parents' divorce, I was exposed to pornography. I didn't have the maturity, understanding, or a parent/mentor to help me sort out my feelings. I just wanted to escape. Porn then wasn't for sexual purposes. I was doing it for emotional release. I learned how to sexualize all my emotions, and I couldn't even define or verbalize the emotions I was feeling.

Proverbs 14:12 says, *"There is a way that appears to be right ..."* If we are honest with our innermost self, there is always a motive for doing what we do. When we willfully disobey God, we have given ourselves a pass or permission to sin. But the second part of this verse says, *"... but in the end, it leads to death."*

✓ How do you handle your emotions? Where are you on the continuum of either denying your emotions or expressing them to everyone you meet? Explain this to the men in your group.

✓ "Porn then wasn't for sexual purposes. I was doing it for emotional release." Do you believe this statement? Why or why not?

We worship our way into an addiction by continually yielding in our hearts to whatever gives us refuge, comfort, and reward. It could be alcohol, drugs, or video games. But in our culture, *porn* and sexual sin have risen to the number one form of worship. To escape this, we must worship our way out of enslavement by focusing our time, energy, money, and hearts on pursuing and glorifying God.

ASSIGNMENT: Memorize Psalm 62:8.

Trust in him at all times, you people; pour out your hearts to him, for God is our refuge. —Psalm 62:8

- ✓ Meditate on Psalm 62:8, using the *Ask Questions* method. Jot down two or three thoughts.

> **Ask Questions**
>
> **Is there:**
>
> A command to obey
>
> A promise to claim
>
> A sin to avoid
>
> An application to make
>
> Something new about God
>
> Ask: Who, What, When, Where, Why
>
> **Emphasize:**
> Different words
>
> **Rewrite**
> In your own words

- ✓ Rewrite Psalm 62:8 in your own words. Be prepared to share this with the group.

- ✓ Record how many times you practiced WWW A MAP over the last four weeks.: _____

Points to Remember

1. God is our ultimate refuge and wants us to express our emotions to Him.

2. Porn addiction is a *worship* issue. We worship our way into porn addiction, and we can worship our way out of its enslavement. Porn trains us to worship a false god.

3. All men have emotions; all have wounded emotions. What we do or how we handle our emotions is key to winning our battle with porn.

✓ To summarize this lesson, write out the most important things you learned.

✓ **Leaders**: Have the men break into pairs and practice WWW A MAP with each other. After one man works through it, have them reverse roles.

Assignment for Next Week

1. Have your Quiet Time this week in the following passages: Proverbs 1:20-33, Colossians 3:5-8, Galatians 5:13-26, and Romans 8:1-8.

2. Try to record five to seven Quiet Times this week. It is okay to use one of your Quiet Times to complete the lesson and one to review verses and work on your current verse.

3. If or when you are tempted this week, ask the Holy Spirit what emotional need you were seeking to meet through porn. Be prepared to share this with your group next week.

4. Place Psalm 62:8 in the front window of your verse pack and memorize it this week.

5. Finish any lessons that you have not completed.

6. Be prepared to share your Every Man A Pure Warrior verses so far.

7. Read through and complete next week's lesson.

Worship

- Start worshiping God by praising Him. Sing your favorite hymn, psalm, or worship song. Offer your body and body parts to God as an act of worship and clothe your body with the armor of God.

Warfare Praying

- First, confess any known sin by praying and say the following spiritual warfare prayer. "Lord Jesus, I ask forgiveness for _____ [name any sin that comes to mind such as looking at porn, masturbation, lust, anger, unforgiveness, greed, or hate]."

- Pray the Lord's Prayer: "Our Father in heaven, hallowed be your name, your kingdom come, your will be done, on earth as it is in heaven. Give us today our daily bread, and forgive us our debts, as we also have forgiven our debtors. And lead us not into temptation, but deliver us from the evil one, for yours is the kingdom and the power and the glory forever. Amen" (Matthew 6:9-13).

- After praying the prayer, personalize it for your temptation. "Lord, please deliver me from the Tempter who is tempting me to _____. Lord, please deliver me from the Accuser who is telling me that my sin is not forgiven." If you are praying with a partner, the partner should say, "I agree in the name of Jesus."

Wounds and Triggers

- Ask the Holy Spirit to show you any wounds that are causing you to act out. Extend forgiveness to anyone who has hurt you. "Lord, I extend forgiveness to_____ for _____."

Amputate

- Separate yourself from any source of porn or lust-inducing environments. If you have just seen a pretty woman who is triggering you, begin to pray for her salvation, that she would find Christ and walk with Him.

Memorize Scripture

- Review your Scripture verses. Begin quoting out loud the verses from Psalm 103, Romans 6, EMAW verses, or any other memorized passages of Scripture.

Allies

- Call a brother for prayer when tempted, confess if you have blown it, and begin to go through these seven principles together.

Preach the Gospel to Yourself Daily

- "I thank You, Father, for the truth that 'there is now no condemnation for those who are in Christ Jesus' (Romans 8:1). I thank You, Jesus, for dying on the cross for me. I praise You that I am forgiven. You look at me as if I had never sinned, and I am adopted into Your family. You purchased me, and now I am free from sin."

LESSON 12
WOUNDS 2: CONNECTING YOUR HEART TO GOD

✓ Have the men break into pairs and recite all their *Every Man A Pure Warrior* verses starting with Psalm 62:8. Have one man hold the cards and say the reference while the other quotes the verse and says the reference at the end of the verse. Then have them switch roles.

✓ Sign off on the *Completion Records*.

✓ Open the session with prayer.

✓ Go around the room, asking each man to share one Quiet Time.

✓ Begin reading the lesson paragraph by paragraph.

✓ Depending on time, have as many men as possible share their *Ask Questions*, meditations and their rewrites of Psalm 86:11.

✓ Read the *Points to Remember* and the *Assignment*.

✓ Break into pairs and practice WWW A MAP with each other. After one man works through it, have them reverse the roles.

This Lesson Further Explains How We Must Recognize Our Emotional Wounds and Connect Our Hearts to God to Escape the Snare of Self-Medicating.

In a previous lesson, I wrote about my dad telling me to stop crying. I promised my dad that I would never cry again. Unfortunately, this damaged *all* my emotions—not just sadness or grief that might lead to crying, but also joy, laughter, and even anger.

Later on, I lived in a house with a stepmom and three sisters. There were numerous fights and emotional outbursts. Emotions were used to manipulate my dad. I saw emotions being turned on and off at will. I saw convincing (feigned) crying in front of a person, only to see laughter the next minute when the person left the room. All these events even further warped my emotions.

When I first looked at porn, my excitement really had nothing to do with sex. It was all damaged emotions that were stirred in my soul which led to the pursuit of porn. I sexualized all emotions. If I felt shame, I'd run to porn. If I felt inadequate or out of control, I'd run to porn. If I felt fear or anxiety, I'd run to porn. If I felt joy, I'd celebrate with porn, lust, and masturbation.

As life goes on, different triggers remind us of our soul's brokenness. There are hundreds of ways we can be "triggered". It could be a smell, our memories, a song, our emotions, or words that remind us of our weakness or woundedness. For me, emotions became the trigger that led to acting out in lust.

When the Holy Spirit revealed the connection between my emotions and my pursuit of porn, it was an "Aha!" moment. It was also the discovery of another key to escape from the prison of porn. I had to reclaim the emotional part of my humanity and bring it under the control and authority of God. I had to yield this part of me to God for healing.

My emotion-ritual-reward cycle could be diagrammed as follows:

THE SEXUAL SIN CYCLE

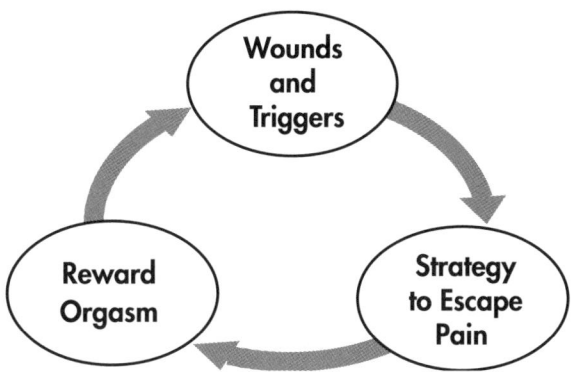

✓ In your own life, what emotions do you feel by looking at porn? Give an example and write a paragraph describing the event when you have run to porn to escape emotions.

✓ Lookup the following verses and state what God says about a hard heart.

Proverbs 28:13-14

Matthew 13:14-15

✓ Look at Ephesians 4:17-19. What is the connection between sensuality and hard, blinded hearts that have lost sensitivity?

✓ Write out several different translations of Ephesians 4:19 for "lost all sensitivity".

✓ Lookup Proverbs 17:20 and Jeremiah 17:9. List the problems of our hearts.

Most men have damaged emotions. When they look at nakedness and indulge in porn, they feel thrilled, enamored, or excited and are entertained. One description of *"enemies of Christ"* in Philippians 3:18-19 is *"their glory is their shame"* because they set their minds on earthly things. Our minds and emotions are warped–we think nakedness is glorious when it is actually shameful.

✓ Lookup the following verses and list the connections between nakedness and the proper emotion you should feel.

Jeremiah 13:26-27

Habakkuk 2:15-16

Revelation 16:15

Outside of marriage, nakedness is shameful and disgraceful and should not be seen as entertainment. But our emotions are warped, so instead of feeling the right emotion of shame, horror and disgrace when we see nakedness, we feel excited and thrilled.

God revealed to me that my emotions were damaged. My dad abandoned our family, leaving my mom alone with five children, and she had cancer. My heart was broken from the feeling that the divorce was my fault and that our family was forever broken.

I was introduced to porn at the age of ten. I immediately found "comfort." I made a vow to my God to never cry again. I bought the lie that showing emotions is unmanly. Porn took over my mind, soul, and affections, further corrupting my heart and darkening my mind.

I joined the military where no emotions except anger were allowed to be expressed.

I took pride in my self-control by never letting anything get to me emotionally. When my wife asked, "Are you going to cry when I die?" I couldn't give her the answer she wanted. I knew that I needed help. I recognized that I possessed a damaged heart, which only God could heal.

So, I asked God for help. If you recognize that your emotions are damaged and need to be realigned to God's emotions, then go through the following process.

Steps to Emotional Healing

Step 1

The first step in emotional recovery is to ask God to teach you about emotions. Ask Him to help you recognize improper feelings. Every person, being made in the image of God, has emotions. Since God has emotions, He experiences delight and pleasure. Psalm 147:11 says, *"... the LORD delights in those who fear him."* He felt that His creation was *"very good"* (Genesis 1:31).

When the Ten Commandments were given, He said, *"You shall have no other gods before me ... for I, the LORD your God, am a jealous God..."* (Exodus 20:3-4). God experienced jealousy. When the people of Israel continued to disobey God, His wrath burned hot. God is also described as having *"zeal"* (Isaiah 9:7). However, God's emotions are pure while ours are corrupted. We should feel pleased with what pleases God and be disgusted with what angers God. See the Appendix for a list of words that express emotional pain. If you are challenged to find words associated with a life wound, this list might help you.

✓ Match the following verses with the emotion expressed to God.

Psalm 25:16	Abandoned or forgotten
Psalm 34:4	Joyful
Psalm 27:9-10	Ashamed
Psalm 31:1	Sorrowful, anguished, and afflicted
Psalm 31:9-10	Fearful
Psalm 4:7	Lonely and overwhelmed

Step 2

The second step in emotional recovery is to ask the Lord to reboot your emotions and realign them with His emotions so you feel the correct emotional response right away.

✓ Read Psalm 86:11. *"Teach me your way, LORD, that I may rely on your faithfulness; give me an undivided heart, that I may fear your name."*
What are the prayer requests of the psalmist?

✓ How does this apply to you and your emotional life?

✓ How emotionally pure is your heart?

Emotions are the gateway to the soul. Once we become aware of emotions in general, we will become aware of the emotional baggage that we are carrying from past hurts and wounds. Until we learn to recognize these deep-seated and sometimes hidden emotions, we won't be able to deal with the wounds of our past that control us in the present. We'll address the healing of wounds in the next lesson.

Step 3

The next step to realign emotions is to learn how to verbalize them to God. As I read through the entire book of Psalms, I am amazed at the depth and breadth of emotions that the psalmists expressed. Not only did they sometimes have these emotions; they talked to God about them. They questioned God's judgment and timing; they were angry at God; they wanted God to take revenge on their enemies, and; they were frustrated at having to wait. They also expressed a love for God and His Word, delight at being in God's presence, and joy in being with the people of God.

You may feel uncomfortable talking to God about your emotions. I grew up in a family in which the only emotion that men expressed was anger. I looked down on men who shared emotions as weak or worse. I had to learn from Scripture and the exhortation of older, godly men to reject the lies I'd believed in my damaged youth. Somehow, theologically, I felt that you were not allowed to talk to God the way David and others talked to God.

✓ Lookup Psalm 62:5-8. How would you describe David's emotional prayer life? How emotionally connected was David with God?

✓ Were emotions discussed in your family? What did you learn from your family about expressing emotions?

✓ Are you comfortable in expressing your feelings to God? Why or why not?

✓ Lookup the following verses: Psalm 42:1-5, 1 Kings 19:3-4 and Jonah 4:1-9. What restrictions, if any, do Scriptures place on sharing our emotions with God?

Step 4

The next step was to learn how to communicate emotions to other people. However, this is fraught with danger. Remember, I had observed emotions being used as weapons. I had to learn a lot of ground rules. Is it safe to share emotions? Who can I trust with my emotions?

Paul encouraged believers in 2 Corinthians 6:11-13 *"We have spoken freely to you, Corinthians, and opened wide our hearts to you. We are not withholding our affection from you, but you are withholding yours from us. As a fair exchange–I speak as to my children–open wide your hearts also."*

✓ Lookup the following verses and record guidelines on expressing emotions to other people.

Ephesians 4:15, 29

Proverbs 29:11

Colossians 4:6

ASSIGNMENT: Memorize Psalm 86:11.

Teach me your way, Lord, that I may rely on your faithfulness; give me an undivided heart, that I may fear your name. —PSALM 86:11

✓ Meditate on Psalm 86:11, using the *Ask Questions* method. Jot down two or three thoughts.

Ask Questions

Is there:

A command to obey

A promise to claim

A sin to avoid

An application to make

Something new about God

Ask: Who, What, When, Where, Why

Emphasize:
Different words

Rewrite
In your own words

✓ Rewrite Psalm 86:11 in your own words. Be prepared to share this with the group.

Points to Remember

1. God made us in His image, and He made us emotional beings.

2. We must grow in understanding our damaged emotions and pouring them out to God.

3. When we disconnect from expressing our emotions to God, we open the door to emotional release in ungodly ways.

4. Godly men are warriors who fight to control and express their emotions in godly ways.

✓ To summarize this lesson, write out the most important things you learned.

✓ Record how many times this week you practiced WWW A MAP: _____

✓ **Leaders**: Have the men break into pairs and practice WWW A MAP with each other. After one man works through it, have them reverse roles.

Assignment for Next Week

1. Review the steps of emotional connectivity with God and others found in this lesson. Read through them several times and then practice them this week.

2. Ask the Lord to search your heart and to reveal emotions that you are stuffing or denying. Ask Him to help you become aware of your emotions. Ask Him to help you live in real-time, sensing and recognizing emotions as they are occurring within you.

3. Try to record five to seven Quiet Times this week in the following passages: Isaiah 53, Matthew 11:28-30, and John 10.

4. Practice the *WAR* method of prayer in your Quiet Times this week. Continue praying for the men in your group to have consistent and quality times with the Lord. Pray against the Enemy's attacking the Quiet Times of the men in the group.

5. Place Psalm 86:11 in the front window of your verse pack and memorize it this week.

6. Finish any lessons that you have not completed.

7. Be prepared to share all your Every Man A Pure Warrior verses.

8. Every day, practice WWW A MAP. At least once this week, call a member of your group and ask him how he is doing in the battle for purity. Use WWW A MAP as a guideline.

9. Read through and complete next week's lesson.

WWW A MAP SEVEN KEYS TO FREEDOM

Worship
- Start worshiping God by praising Him. Sing your favorite hymn, psalm, or worship song. Offer your body and body parts to God as an act of worship and clothe your body with the armor of God.

Warfare Praying
- First, confess any known sin by praying and say the following spiritual warfare prayer. "Lord Jesus, I ask forgiveness for _____ [name any sin that comes to mind such as looking at porn, masturbation, lust, anger, unforgiveness, greed, or hate]."
- Pray the Lord's Prayer: "Our Father in heaven, hallowed be your name, your kingdom come, your will be done, on earth as it is in heaven. Give us today our daily bread, and forgive us our debts, as we also have forgiven our debtors. And lead us not into temptation, but deliver us from the evil one, for yours is the kingdom and the power and the glory forever. Amen" (Matthew 6:9-13).
- After praying the prayer, personalize it for your temptation. "Lord, please deliver me from the Tempter who is tempting me to _____. Lord, please deliver me from the Accuser who is telling me that my sin is not forgiven." If you are praying with a partner, the partner should say, "I agree in the name of Jesus."

Wounds and Triggers
- Ask the Holy Spirit to show you any wounds that are causing you to act out. Extend forgiveness to anyone who has hurt you. "Lord, I extend forgiveness to_____ for _____."

Amputate
- Separate yourself from any source of porn or lust-inducing environments. If you have just seen a pretty woman who is triggering you, begin to pray for her salvation, that she would find Christ and walk with Him.

Memorize Scripture
- Review your Scripture verses. Begin quoting out loud the verses from Psalm 103, Romans 6, EMAW verses, or any other memorized passages of Scripture.

Allies
- Call a brother for prayer when tempted, confess if you have blown it, and begin to go through these seven principles together.

Preach the Gospel to Yourself Daily
- "I thank You, Father, for the truth that 'there is now no condemnation for those who are in Christ Jesus' (Romans 8:1). I thank You, Jesus, for dying on the cross for me. I praise You that I am forgiven. You look at me as if I had never sinned, and I am adopted into Your family. You purchased me, and now I am free from sin."

LESSON 13
WOUNDS 3: FORGIVENESS—REMOVING THE THORN OF WOUNDEDNESS

- ✓ Have the men break into pairs and recite all their *Every Man A Pure Warrior* verses to each other, beginning with Psalm 86:11. Have one man hold the cards and say the reference while the other quotes the verse and says the reference at the end of the verse. Then have them switch roles.

- ✓ Sign off on the *Completion Records*.

- ✓ Open the session with prayer.

- ✓ Go around the room, asking each man to share one Quiet Time.

- ✓ Begin reading the lesson paragraph by paragraph.

- ✓ Depending on time, have as many men as possible share their *Ask Questions*, meditations and their rewrites of Isaiah 53:4-5.

- ✓ Read the *Points to Remember* and the *Assignment*.

- ✓ Break into pairs and practice WWW A MAP with each other. After one man works through it, have them reverse the roles.

This Lesson Explains How We Must Forgive Those Who Have Wounded Us, in Order to Escape the Cycle of Pursuing Ungodly Practices.

Healing for Wounds: Brandon's Story

Brandon was new to EMAW and showed promise of becoming a fruitful disciple. He was faithful to complete the assignments each week, was always on time, and was eager to share his findings from his previous week's study.

When it came time for sharing, he was relatively open and honest. He was struggling with lust, porn, and masturbation, and he had on occasion visited prostitutes. He was memorizing Scriptures regularly and fervently. He wanted to be free from enslavement to sexual sin.

As I spent time getting to know Brandon, I learned that there had been significant trauma in his early life. He loved and idolized his dad. His dad was cool in his eyes, rode a motorcycle, had cool friends, and had tattoos. Then one day, without notice, the police knocked on the door of their house, and his dad was taken away in handcuffs. He was charged with murder and was sent away to prison for life, with minimal possibility of parole.

Brandon was devastated. Their family had drastically changed overnight. His mom tried holding it together, but money was tight, and they had to move to a cheaper place. Then they moved several more times. Brandon's mom was working several jobs, and Brandon was left alone much of the time. His mom took Brandon to see his dad in prison several times the first year, but because his dad was jailed four to five hours away from where they lived, they couldn't visit him very often. After a couple of years, he never saw his dad again. Then, a few years later, he noticed his mom was having significant mood swings. She had turned to drugs and alcohol to deaden her pain. One night, she overdosed and died. She had left a suicide note but the police would not let him read it. Brandon was sent to foster care and lived in a number of homes until he reached adulthood.

When he was seven or eight, Brandon saw his first adult video. He soon learned how to masturbate, and before long he was habitually touching himself. While in college he heard the gospel and gave his life to Jesus. He became involved in a discipleship group and was growing, but his chronic consumption of porn and all that came with it was normal and acceptable to him now. He said, "I don't even think about it. When I feel the slightest emotion, whatever that emotion is, I just look for a place to relieve myself and press on with life. It's just a habit."

I asked him, "What impact do you think the absence of your father and your mother has had on you?"

Brandon quickly replied, "None." He went on to say rather forcefully, "I'm my own man. I make my own choices. All that crap happened in my past and has nothing to do with me now."

I challenged him. "I think you are both right and wrong about this. You are right in that you are your own man and you make your own choices, and you are right in that you will be held accountable for your choices. But I think your father's and mother's abandonment of you by his going to jail and her suicide has deeply affected your thinking and your outlook on life and is directly contributing to your failings in your pursuit of purity."

The incarceration of his dad and the death of his mother severely wounded Brandon. He turned to lust, porn, masturbation, and prostitutes as Band-Aids, seeking sexual release to deaden the pain of feeling abandoned.

✓ *"When I feel the slightest emotion, whatever that emotion is, I just look for a place to relieve myself and press on with life. It's just a habit."* What do you think of Brandon's statement? Does this happen to you? Explain.

> ✓ **Leaders:** Read the following instructions to the group or the listening, healing prayer exercise. Have one man volunteer to go through the steps outlined in the listening, healing prayer process.

HEALING PRAYER, LISTENING PRAYER

To heal our wounds, there is a general process to follow.

    1. Recognize that you are wounded. Some review the wound every day. They talk about it to themselves, reliving the offense, playing the wounding conversations over and over in their minds. Some tell others every chance they get how they've been wronged.

2. Seek out an intercessor, friend, pastor, or counselor. Most people who have deep-seated wounds and habits of sin need the help of someone who is trusted and mature. For some people, the wounds are so deep that they've buried them in their subconscious, or they have disassociated themselves from the pain to merely survive. In this case, professional counselors are invaluable. I actively encouraged Brandon to see an excellent Christian counselor to release his denial of the impact of his mother's death and his father's separation from their family.

✓ Leaders:

- In step 4, the volunteer should express to God the wound or trauma that he experienced. All the other men should be in prayer with and for the volunteer. As he talks to God about the wound, the leader should be listening intently and taking notes.

- In steps 5, 6, and 7, the volunteer should express to God his emotions surrounding the trauma, such as anger, hatred, rage, betrayal, and fear. After telling God his emotions, he should own his negative emotions that are sinful. These could include: hatred toward the person causing the wound. After confessing his sinful emotions, lead him into a prayer of forgiveness for the person or persons who caused the wound. The leader should guide the man to verbalize what he currently feels about himself and about God.

- In step 8, after the volunteer verbalizes his emotions and statements that he considers to be true: such as "I'm a loser," enter into a time of silence, asking God to speak to the volunteer. In prayer, ask God if these statements are true, such as "Am I a loser, God?" If you are doing this the first time as a leader, it may seem weird and awkward. The Holy Spirit *does* want to speak to us and minister to us in our deepest areas of woundedness. *After a time of silence, ask the volunteer to report any scriptures or thoughts that comes to mind.*

3. **Practice listening prayer.** Romans 8:16 says *"When we cry, 'Abba! Father!' it is the Spirit himself bearing witness with our spirit that we are children of God (RSVCE)."* We can humbly come before Jesus with our hurts and ask Him to speak to us. It's best to do this with someone more mature and experienced in listening prayer. As we enter into prayer, we start with a short time of praise and worship.

4. **Ask Jesus to reveal Himself during your trauma.** In Brandon's case, he could ask, "Jesus, where were You when my father left? What were You feeling? How should I look at this? What lie am I believing that is associated with this trauma? Do You have a word for me? Will you please reveal Yourself to me? When I was a little boy, about to be without a father for the rest of my life, what was I feeling? Please reveal to me the anguish of my heart." God is not limited by time. He created time. He existed before time and will exist after time ceases. So He totally understands our past traumas and can help us deal with them.

5. **If you are aware of any emotions surrounding the trauma, express them to God.** Tell God things such as: "I was angry," "I felt out of control," "I was confused," "I was worried," "I was afraid," "I was hurt," "I felt betrayed," "I felt powerless," "I felt stupid."

6. **Confess and forgive.** Some of these emotions, however understandable and normal, could have devolved into sin. If your hurt has turned into hatred, resentment, and bitterness, own those feelings, confess them as sin and ask God for forgiveness.

The hardest part of this whole process is to obey Jesus and forgive those who have wounded us. As we forgive those who have wounded us, we enter into a greater sense of the sufferings of Jesus. Forgiveness is always an act of the will, *not* our emotions. It's a choice we make out of our love for Jesus, following his example. He was being unjustly crucified yet in His dying breaths He prayed, *"Father, forgive them, for they do not know what they are doing"* found in Luke 23:34.

We also are to obey His commands found in Colossians 3:8-10, 13.

✓ **Leaders**: Have someone read these Colossians verses.

7. **Satan is a master of taking our negative emotions from our wounds and whispering lies to us.** He'll tell us lies about God and he'll tell us lies

about us. Verbalize what you believe about yourself or about God as a result of the trauma. It could be lies such as: "I am worthless," "I am tainted," "I am unloved," "I am a loser," "I'm a nobody," "I'm insignificant," "I can never do anything right," "You are powerless," "You don't care," "You are unapproachable."

8. **Satan is a slanderer.** Pray and ask the Lord if any of the statements found at the end of #7 are true. Ask the Lord, "Am I worthless?", or "Am I powerless?". Whatever negative statements you have been telling yourself, ask the Lord if these are true.

Then, in silence, you and your prayer partner can wait for the Lord to speak or to reveal Himself. The prerequisite is to make sure there are no unconfessed sins and that as far as you know, you are right with God. Many times, the Lord will bring Scripture to mind. Sometimes He might bring a picture to mind. He might allow you to see a look on His face, perhaps tears or sadness. Others have reported that Jesus stood with open arms and invited them to sit on His lap.

These are compelling moments of healing. When the Lord reveals to you a word, a phrase, a verse, or a picture, that is a sacred time. You realize that you were not alone, and not abandoned when you experienced that earlier trauma. You realize that God was there all along. Many times, His presence or the awareness of His presence acts as a supernatural healing balm. A change of perspective occurs, an attitude adjustment. This is what Asaph recorded in Psalm 73:16-28. Other times God may reveal a hidden truth. That truth may be an ugly reality, but it sets you free from the lies and misconceptions you held dear. In the midst of this unpleasantness, you sense God's powerful presence and comfort.

✓ **Leaders**: Have someone read Psalm 73:16-28 out loud. Note how the psalmist's attitude changed by being in the presence of God.

9. **Praise.** Enter into a time of worship and blessing God. This has been a holy moment of encounter with the Lord Jesus. He is the Great Shepherd and the Guardian of our souls.

10. **Repeat as needed and as often as you become aware of different wounds.** I've repeated this process numerous times, whenever I become aware of a barrier with someone or when something triggers a desire to run to my old way of handling stresses.

God Wants to Heal Our Deepest Wounds.

Dan, a young believer, was in a training program, learning how to share the gospel and lead folks to Jesus. In the course of his training, he stood up in front of forty people and gave his testimony of how he became a Christian. He was scared to death. It was the first time he had ever spoken publicly. Dan told everyone that his dad had sexually abused him when he was a young boy. Then he added, "And I will *never* forgive him."

His emotions were understandable and reasonable.

One of the younger, immature believers walked up to him and casually but forcefully said, "You know, you're going to have to forgive your dad if you want to keep growing as a believer."

Dan yelled at this brother, saying, "I will *never* forgive him!"

He walked out of the training program and broke fellowship with that group of believers. The pain of the wound was too raw; he was too hurt to receive any counsel or help. He was not ready to deal with the pain.

✓ How does John 16:12 relate to the encounter Dan had with his friend?

Even though the young believer was right in what he said to Dan, it was not said at the right time. Someone has described truth as a heavy weight. Every bridge has a load limit. If the weight is too much, the bridge could collapse. We should work toward a relationship that is solid enough to bear the weight of truth.

Several months later Dan came back into the fellowship. He worked through the steps of listening, healing prayer. When he asked Jesus to speak to him and to reveal where He was when Dan was being abused by his dad, a clear picture came into Dan's mind of Jesus weeping. Dan was overwhelmed with sadness, grief, and the emotion of feeling understood by Jesus. He had *not* been abandoned. God gave Dan the strength and grace to forgive his abusive father.

Jesus is more than able to carry our wounds. He was severely wounded for us. He suffered rejection from the Father because He was bearing the weight of our sin. The very people He created rejected Him. His disciples, with whom He had spent three years, denied Him, running away from Him during His time of need. His brothers mocked Him. He died alone and abandoned for us. He knows all about rejection and wounding. Everything that we have experienced in the way of suffering, Jesus has suffered.

Yet even at the height of His suffering, when He was dying on the cross, Jesus forgave His attackers. He prayed, *"Father, forgive them, for they do not know what they are doing"* (Luke 23:34). Forgiveness is not optional for a believer. We are *commanded* to forgive those who have hurt and wounded us, just as Christ has freely forgiven us.

ASSIGNMENT: Memorize Isaiah 53:4-5.

Surely he took up our pain and bore our suffering, yet we considered him punished by God, stricken by him, and afflicted. But he was pierced for our transgressions, he was crushed for our iniquities; the punishment that brought us peace was on him, and by his wounds we are healed.

—Isaiah 53:4-5

✓ Meditate on Isaiah 53:4-5, using the *Ask Questions* method. Jot down two or three thoughts.

Ask Questions

Is there:

A command to obey

A promise to claim

A sin to avoid

An application to make

Something new about God

Ask: Who, What, When, Where, Why

Emphasize:
Different words

Rewrite
In your own words

✓ Rewrite Isaiah 53:4-5 in your own words. Be prepared to share this with the group.

Points to Remember

1. All of us have wounds. Our normal, fleshly reaction is to run from pain. We will find some Band-Aid to try to stop the hurt.

2. Unhealed wounds provide an open door to pornography or other addictive practices.

3. We must recognize our wounds and our reactions to our wounds and bring them to Jesus for healing.

4. Jesus can heal our deepest wounds. He longs to touch us and speak to us.

5. We are commanded to seek forgiveness and to forgive those who have wounded us in order to receive healing.

✓ To summarize this lesson, write out the most important things you learned.

✓ Record how many times this week you practiced WWW A MAP:
_____

✓ **Leaders**: Have the men break into pairs and practice WWW A MAP with each other. After one man works through it, have them reverse roles.

Assignment for Next Week

Review the steps of listening, healing prayer found in this lesson. Read them several times and practice them this week.

1. Ask the Lord to search your heart for any barriers or past wounds that are holding back your growth.

2. Set aside time this week and work through the process of listening, healing prayer. Be prepared to share with your group next week what the Lord revealed to you through this process.

3. Try to record five to seven Quiet Times this week in the following passages: Genesis 39, 1 Corinthians 6:18-20, and Acts 19.

4. Practice the *WAR* method of prayer in your Quiet Times this week. Continue praying for the men in your group to have consistent quality times with the Lord. Pray against the Enemy's attacking the Quiet Times of the men in the group.

5. Place Isaiah 53:4-5 in the front window of your verse pack and memorize it this week.

6. Finish any lessons that you have not completed.

7. Be prepared to share all your Every Man A Pure Warrior verses.

8. Every day, practice WWW A MAP. At least once this week, call a member of your group and ask him how he is doing in the battle for purity. Use WWW A MAP as a guideline.

9. Read through and complete next week's lesson.

Worship

- Start worshiping God by praising Him. Sing your favorite hymn, psalm, or worship song. Offer your body and body parts to God as an act of worship and clothe your body with the armor of God.

Warfare Praying

- First, confess any known sin by praying and say the following spiritual warfare prayer. "Lord Jesus, I ask forgiveness for _____ [name any sin that comes to mind such as looking at porn, masturbation, lust, anger, unforgiveness, greed, or hate]."

- Pray the Lord's Prayer: "Our Father in heaven, hallowed be your name, your kingdom come, your will be done, on earth as it is in heaven. Give us today our daily bread, and forgive us our debts, as we also have forgiven our debtors. And lead us not into temptation, but deliver us from the evil one, for yours is the kingdom and the power and the glory forever. Amen" (Matthew 6:9-13).

- After praying the prayer, personalize it for your temptation. "Lord, please deliver me from the Tempter who is tempting me to _____. Lord, please deliver me from the Accuser who is telling me that my sin is not forgiven." If you are praying with a partner, the partner should say, "I agree in the name of Jesus."

Wounds and Triggers

- Ask the Holy Spirit to show you any wounds that are causing you to act out. Extend forgiveness to anyone who has hurt you. "Lord, I extend forgiveness to_____ for _____."

Amputate

- Separate yourself from any source of porn or lust-inducing environments. If you have just seen a pretty woman who is triggering you, begin to pray for her salvation, that she would find Christ and walk with Him.

Memorize Scripture

- Review your Scripture verses. Begin quoting out loud the verses from Psalm 103, Romans 6, EMAW verses, or any other memorized passages of Scripture.

Allies

- Call a brother for prayer when tempted, confess if you have blown it, and begin to go through these seven principles together.

Preach the Gospel to Yourself Daily

- "I thank You, Father, for the truth that 'there is now no condemnation for those who are in Christ Jesus' (Romans 8:1). I thank You, Jesus, for dying on the cross for me. I praise You that I am forgiven. You look at me as if I had never sinned, and I am adopted into Your family. You purchased me, and now I am free from sin."

LESSON 14
AMPUTATION AND BLOCKADE

✓ Have the men break into pairs and recite all their Every Man A Pure Warrior verses to each other, beginning with Isaiah 53:4-5. Have one man hold the cards and say the reference while the other quotes the verse and says the reference at the end of the verse. Then have them switch roles.

   ✓ Sign off on the *Completion Records*.

   ✓ Open the session with prayer.

   ✓ Go around the room, asking each man to share one Quiet Time.

   ✓ Begin reading the lesson paragraph by paragraph.

   ✓ Depending on time, have as many men as possible share their *Ask Questions*, meditations, and rewrites of 1 Corinthians 6:18-20.

   ✓ Read the *Points to Remember* and the *Assignment*.

   ✓ Break into pairs and practice WWW A MAP with each other. After one man works through it, have them reverse the roles.

This Lesson Explains "Radical Amputation" and the Ongoing Need to Block Pornography From Our Lives.

Terry's Story: "I Have a Sledgehammer"

I had the privilege of leading Terry to Christ. He was single, a little older than me, and enslaved to pornography. As he grew, spending time in the Word, he kept hitting roadblocks that prevented his spiritual growth.

Talking to him on the phone one day, I asked him, "Have you gotten rid of all the porn in your house?" He hesitated with his answer, and that was a dead giveaway that he still had some porn. He finally said, "I have some DVDs in the garage." I asked him, "How many?" He said, "A padded notebook full."

I explained to him the importance of getting rid of *all* porn and *all* access to porn. I call that radical amputation. Jesus said, *"... if your eye causes you to stumble, pluck it out"* (Matthew 5:27-30). I told Terry, "You must get rid of all that poison." He agreed and said he would immediately destroy the porn.

I felt a prompting in my spirit to help him and to ensure that he followed through with his pledge. My schedule was open, so I said, "I have some time, and I have a sledgehammer. I'd love to come over and help you destroy your porn." He was overjoyed and incredulous. He said, "Would you really come and help me?" I assured him that I would be delighted.

Twenty minutes later I arrived at his house and was surprised. He had not just one notebook full of DVDs, but five of them, each holding one-hundred pornographic DVDs. Each DVD averaged six hours in length. He had more than three thousand hours of videos that he had collected and intended on watching.

As we laid the videos on the ground and swung our sledgehammers down, smashing the DVDs, Terry confided in me, "I've been watching one video every day since I've been retired!"

- ✓ Hyperbole is used in every language to illustrate truth with exaggeration. Read Matthew 18:8-9 and discuss what Jesus said about the need for radical amputation of sin in your life.

The world's systems (entertainment, fashion, education, and financial) are designed to meet our needs apart from God. We live, work, and minister within these world systems, but we are not to conform to them. Jesus taught that although we are in this world, we are not supposed to be of this world.

- ✓ Acts 19:17-20 records the story of how many people in the city of Ephesus turned away from their idols and turned instead to the worship of Jesus. Summarize what they did to radically amputate or separate themselves from sin.

Paul, in 1 Corinthians 5, also dealt with the issue of immorality within the church. A man was sleeping with his father's wife. The church in Corinth prided itself on its tolerance, but Paul sharply rebuked that church. He admonished and instructed that church to separate the immoral man from the body of Christ and treat him as an unbeliever. It was a form of radical amputation for the purity of the church. This man was a brother in Christ who was living in open, unconfessed sin.

In verses 9-11 of 1 Corinthians 5, Paul says, "*I wrote to you in my letter not to associate with sexually immoral people—not at all meaning the people of this world who are immoral, or the greedy and swindlers, or idolaters. In that case, you would have to leave this world. But now I am writing to you that you must not associate with anyone who claims to be a brother or sister but is sexually immoral or greedy, an idolater or slanderer, a drunkard or swindler. Do not even eat with such people.*"

- ✓ Which step of church discipline from Matthew 18 does 1 Corinthians 5 represent?

The Scriptures are clear: we live in the world and need to associate with the "immoral" people of the world, to influence them and possibly lead them to salvation in Jesus. But also we must remain true to Christ. So far this study has looked at amputating sinful practices and dealing with sinful people in your life. Now we are turning to isolating, blocking or blockading sinful practices from entering your life.

✓ Read 1 Corinthians 9:19-27 three or four times and write a paragraph about the need for self-control in order to block sinful practices from entering your life.

Every day, we make hundreds of choices about how we will live our lives. When we are not working or studying, each day we have minutes or hours of discretionary time. How we choose to spend those minutes or hours will determine the quality of our walk with God and potentially our fruitfulness and whether or not we will succeed in life.

We make choices about how much TV to watch. We choose which movies to view and how long we listen to music. We select our friends. We decide what to read. We decide where and how we spend our money. We choose whether to meet with God for a Quiet Time each day. We decide whether to carry our verses with us to review and meditate. We determine what routes we take to work. These "little" choices that we make throughout the day reveal our understanding of and commitment to what it means to *"love the Lord your God with all your heart and with all your soul and with all your mind"* (Matthew 22:37).

I have made choices to separate from porn and all access to porn within my home and my electronics. My wife maintains the parental control codes for the TV. I've installed filters on my computers and my phone. These choices are available for all of us. As believers in a sex-saturated, porn-saturated world, we *must* take steps to guard our eyes and our paths.

✓ Most if not all technology allows you to limit access to adult material. It may be called something like "Safe Search", or "Parental Controls". There are a number of filters available to both block and or report your activities to a friend of your choice. Some of the companies which provide these filters are listed in Lesson 3 on Allies. If you have yet to install such a blocking device, do so this week and report it to your allies. Allies, ask your friend if he has followed through on blockading porn from his electronic devices.

✓ Turn "Restricted Mode" on for YouTube, if you have not already done so. Click your profile picture, and then select Restricted Mode. In the dialog box that appears, toggle Restricted Mode to "on".

The Lord always appeals to both our will and our intellect so we can be prudent in our dealings with the world while at the same time engaging the world with the gospel. We are to be wise and avoid situations in which we could become defiled or the gospel could be discredited.

✓ Read Genesis 39:1-23, the story of Joseph and his extreme challenge regarding sexual temptation. Write down what impresses you about Joseph's character.

One of the fundamental principles in winning the battle for sexual purity is the flee principle. Joseph ran from the immediate temptation presented by Potiphar's wife. This Old Testament hero of the faith modeled for us a vital New Testament teaching, and he suffered for his obedience, only to be rewarded later by God.

The reality is that with our current climate of unlimited, available, free pornography, we live in a modern-day Sodom and Gomorrah. Yet in the midst of all this debauchery, God still calls us to live holy lives, and He *"... has given us everything we need for a godly life ..."* (2 Peter 1:3).

✓ Lookup the following three passages. Notice the command to flee sexual temptation. Highlight the parts you should amputate and the parts you should blockade.

1 Corinthians 6:18-20

2 Timothy 2:20-22

Romans 13:12-14

✓ Take a quick inventory of your life. Have you amputated all porn and blocked access to porn from your living environment? What do you still need to amputate and/or blockade from your life?

✓ Write a summary of what you have learned about being in the world but not of the world and about keeping yourself from being stained by the world. Be prepared to share this with the group.

ASSIGNMENT: Memorize 1 Corinthians 6:18-20.

Flee from sexual immorality. All other sins a person commits are outside the body, but whoever sins sexually, sins against their own body. Do you not know that your bodies are temples of the Holy Spirit, who is in you, whom you have received from God? You are not your own; you were bought at a price. Therefore honor God with your bodies. —1 CORINTHIANS 6:18-20

✓ Meditate on 1 Corinthians 6:18-20, using the *Ask Questions* method. Jot down two or three thoughts.

> **Ask Questions**
>
> **Is there:**
>
> A command to obey
>
> A promise to claim
>
> A sin to avoid
>
> An application to make
>
> Something new about God
>
> Ask: Who, What, When, Where, Why
>
> **Emphasize:**
> Different words
>
> **Rewrite**
> In your own words

✓ Rewrite 1 Corinthians 6:18-20 in your own words. Be prepared to share this with the group.

Points to Remember

1. Though we live in the world, we are not of the world. We are to keep ourselves from being morally stained by the world (James 1:27).

2. There are times when we must flee from temptation while running toward Jesus.

3. If we are caught in any sin, particularly sexual immorality, we are to do whatever is necessary to radically amputate or remove the sin. We also have to destroy whatever porn we possess and block or blockade our ability to access more easily.

✓ To summarize this lesson, write out the most important things you learned.

✓ Record how many times this week you practiced WWW A MAP: _____

✓ **Leaders**: Have the men break into pairs and practice WWW A MAP with each other. After one man works through it, have them reverse roles.

Assignment for Next Week

1. For your Quiet Times this week, please focus on the following verses: Isaiah 53, Romans 5:9, Ephesians 1:7, Hebrews 13:12, and 1 John 1:7. Take one verse each day and meditate on it.

2. Try to record three to five Quiet Times this week. It is okay to use one of your Quiet Times to complete the lesson and one to review the verses or just sing praise and worship songs to the Lord.

3. Practice the *WAR* method of prayer in your Quiet Times this week. Continue praying for the men in your group to have consistent and quality times with the Lord. Pray against the Enemy's attacking the Quiet Times of the men in the

4. Place 1 Corinthians 6:18-20 in the front window of your verse pack and memorize it this week.

5. Finish any lessons that you have not completed.

6. Be prepared to share all your Every Man A Pure Warrior verses.

7. Every day, practice WWW A MAP. At least once this week call a member of your group and ask him how he is doing in the battle for purity. Use WWW A MAP as a guideline.

8. Read through and complete next week's lesson.

Worship

- Start worshiping God by praising Him. Sing your favorite hymn, psalm, or worship song. Offer your body and body parts to God as an act of worship and clothe your body with the armor of God.

Warfare Praying

- First, confess any known sin by praying and say the following spiritual warfare prayer. "Lord Jesus, I ask forgiveness for _____ [name any sin that comes to mind such as looking at porn, masturbation, lust, anger, unforgiveness, greed, or hate]."

- Pray the Lord's Prayer: "Our Father in heaven, hallowed be your name, your kingdom come, your will be done, on earth as it is in heaven. Give us today our daily bread, and forgive us our debts, as we also have forgiven our debtors. And lead us not into temptation, but deliver us from the evil one, for yours is the kingdom and the power and the glory forever. Amen" (Matthew 6:9-13).

- After praying the prayer, personalize it for your temptation. "Lord, please deliver me from the Tempter who is tempting me to _____. Lord, please deliver me from the Accuser who is telling me that my sin is not forgiven." If you are praying with a partner, the partner should say, "I agree in the name of Jesus."

Wounds and Triggers

- Ask the Holy Spirit to show you any wounds that are causing you to act out. Extend forgiveness to anyone who has hurt you. "Lord, I extend forgiveness to _____ for _____."

Amputate

- Separate yourself from any source of porn or lust-inducing environments. If you have just seen a pretty woman who is triggering you, begin to pray for her salvation, that she would find Christ and walk with Him.

Memorize Scripture

- Review your Scripture verses. Begin quoting out loud the verses from Psalm 103, Romans 6, EMAW verses, or any other memorized passages of Scripture.

Allies

- Call a brother for prayer when tempted, confess if you have blown it, and begin to go through these seven principles together.

Preach the Gospel to Yourself Daily

- "I thank You, Father, for the truth that 'there is now no condemnation for those who are in Christ Jesus' (Romans 8:1). I thank You, Jesus, for dying on the cross for me. I praise You that I am forgiven. You look at me as if I had never sinned, and I am adopted into Your family. You purchased me, and now I am free from sin."

LESSON 15
PREACH THE GOSPEL TO YOURSELF DAILY

- ✓ Have the men break into pairs and recite all their Every Man A Pure Warrior verses to each other, beginning with 1 Corinthians 6:18-20. Have one man hold the card and say the reference while the other quotes the verse and says the reference at the end of the verse. Then have them switch roles.

- ✓ Sign off on the *Completion Records*.

- ✓ Open the session with prayer.

- ✓ Go around the room, asking each man to share one Quiet Time.

- ✓ Begin reading the lesson paragraph by paragraph.

- ✓ Depending on time, have as many men as possible share their *Ask Questions*, meditations and their rewrites of 2 Corinthians 11:3 and Galatians 2:20.

- ✓ Read the *Points to Remember* and the *Assignment*.

- ✓ Break into pairs and practice WWW A MAP with each other. After one man works through it, have them reverse the roles.

Finally, We Must Keep Our First Love by Preaching the Gospel to Ourselves Daily.

Jesus warned the church in Ephesus in Revelation 2:4 that they allowed their "first love" of him to grow cold. Porn will pull you away from loving Jesus. Therefore, you need to keep reminding yourself of the gospel and keep your love of Jesus vibrant.

Noted Navigators author Jerry Bridges, in his book *The Discipline of Grace*, coined the phrase "preaching the gospel to yourself." It means daily sitting at the cross of Jesus and reviewing all the incredible spiritual truths that are found in and through the sacrifice of Jesus and His dying on our behalf. It means every day reminding ourselves who we are before Christ, what Christ has done for us, and how that has fundamentally changed our identities.

One famous, American, daytime TV host focused an episode of her show on the male sex drive. The question on that show was, "How often does a healthy man think about sex?" Her panel of experts concluded, about one sexual thought every seven seconds!

At one of my seminars, a man came to me and said, "I decided to do a little mathematics and estimate how many sexual sins I've committed over the course of my life. I gave myself grace, and instead of using the once-every-seven-seconds criteria, I figured I was having an impure thought once every five minutes. Estimating twelve impure thoughts per hour times being awake eighteen hours per day times 365 days per year times thirty years of consuming porn equals over two million sinful, sexual thoughts. That's not counting all the sins of gossip, slander, hatred, disrespect toward authorities, breaking the law, dishonoring parents, and every other quantifiable sin I've committed. That's a lot of sin–millions and millions of sins. And that is just my sin. Now multiply that by the population of the world, and it's overwhelming the total number of sins that were put on Christ at the cross." Amen! Billy Graham said, "Be assured that there is no sin that you have ever committed that the blood of Jesus cannot cleanse."

✓ Read Isaiah 53:6-10. Underline the words that speak of the punishment that Christ received for our sins.

We all, like sheep, have gone astray,
    each of us has turned to our own way;
and the Lord has laid on him
    the iniquity of us all.

He was oppressed and afflicted,
    yet he did not open his mouth;
he was led like a lamb to the slaughter,
    and as a sheep before its shearers is silent,
    so he did not open his mouth.

By oppression and judgment he was taken away.
    Yet who of his generation protested?
For he was cut off from the land of the living;
    for the transgression of my people he was punished.
He was assigned a grave with the wicked,
    and with the rich in his death,
though he had done no violence,
    nor was any deceit in his mouth.

Yet it was the Lord's will to crush him and cause him to suffer,
    and though the Lord makes his life an offering for sin,
he will see his offspring and prolong his days,
    and the will of the Lord will prosper in his hand.

                                            —Isaiah 53:6-10

✓ Read Isaiah 52:14. If you were a reporter and you arrived at the scene of the crucifixion right after Jesus died, how would you describe the body of Jesus to your readers?

✓ Read Romans 5:6-10. How has Jesus' death affected our standing with God?

Colossians 2:13-14 says, *"When you were dead in your sins and the uncircumcision of your flesh, God made you alive with Christ. He forgave us all our sins, having canceled the charge of our legal indebtedness, which stood against us and condemned us; he has taken it away, nailing it to the cross."* By Jesus' sacrifice on the cross, all my millions of sins were forgiven. His life and sacrificial death washed me of all my sins.

✓ Read the story of the sinful woman who was forgiven in Luke 7:36-50. Why was the woman so grateful?

When I think about this story, I'm reminded of how many of my sins the Lord has forgiven. Note what Jesus said about the sinful woman who washed His feet with her tears and anointed Him with perfume: *"... her many sins have been forgiven—as her great love has shown"* (Luke 7:47). How much more should I love Jesus and be devoted to Him, even extravagant in my praise and worship of Him!

Christianity was born out of Judaism which practiced animal sacrifices. The "blood" of Christ shed on the cross is a graphic metaphor for the sacrificial death of Jesus as the lamb of God to cover sin. It is not a mystical substance but a historical event which brought about the redemption of mankind. Note precisely what we have gained, or received, because of His sacrificial death.

✓ Lookup the following four verses that speak of the precious blood of Jesus.

Ephesians 1:7

Romans 5:9

1 John 1:7

Hebrews 13:12

I am not ashamed of the gospel, because it is the power of God that brings salvation to everyone who believes: first to the Jew, then to the Gentile. —Romans 1:16

✓ Write down your definition of the following five terms associated with the blood of Jesus. Use a dictionary as needed.

Redemption

Forgiveness

Justification

Sanctification

Cleansing

These five theological concepts are foundational to our understanding of the gospel. They encourage us when we're down, strengthen us when we're weak, and energize us when we're lazy. They form the basis of who we are. They also form the basis of worship of and devotion to our Savior.

✓ Lookup Revelation 12:7-12. What spiritual weapons used to overcome Satan are mentioned in this passage?

✓ **Leaders**: Pray as a group. Have each person vocalize praise and worship, mentioning the sacrificial death of Jesus and each truth separately: redemption, the forgiveness of sins, justification, sanctification, and cleansing of sin.

Jesus' death, burial, and resurrection is the pivotal event in world history. It satisfies the wrath of God for sin. Jesus' blood purchases us, paying the redemption price for sin. The act of our conversion transfers us from the dominion of darkness into the kingdom of Jesus. When we come to faith, we become a new creation, adopted into the family of God, and certified as a citizen of heaven. We are washed, forgiven, sealed by God, and given His Spirit to live inside us. We also become a partaker and recipient of the grace of God. John 1:17 says that grace and truth come through Jesus Christ.

Grace is a gift from God that we do not deserve. Grace is the supernatural energy that God gives us to obey him. The battle for holiness and purity is impossible apart from the grace of God. When we are facing temptation, we need grace, God's power to resist. When or if we blow it, we need grace, the energy to get back up and resume the fight.

✓ Lookup John 1:14-17 and Hebrews 4:15-16. How does a person receive grace?

✓ Get into the habit of preaching the gospel to yourself every day. Pray something like the following:

Jesus, I worship and praise You today. I thank You for dying for me on the cross. Thank You for voluntarily shedding Your blood for me. It's through Your blood that I have been redeemed. You have purchased me and paid the ransom for me, and now I am free from bondage and delivered from the dominion of darkness.

I praise You that Your blood has justified me. I have been given the righteousness of Christ. All the legal demands that were on me because of my innumerable sins have been nailed to the cross, set aside because of Your sacrifice. I praise You that through Your blood, You have sanctified me, making me holy. You have adopted me, making me part of Your eternal family. You have made me a citizen of Your kingdom. You have also made me Your ambassador and have given me a holy mission to make You known in the world.

I praise You that Your blood forgives me. I am released from the debt of my sin. I praise You for Your absolute pardon and forgiveness. Father, I praise and worship You for continuing to cleanse me of all my sins. I could not even approach You apart from the blood of Jesus. I praise You for the gospel, the tremendous news of salvation and deliverance found in the death, burial, and resurrection of Jesus Christ.

We need to quiet our inner man and sit at Jesus' feet as Mary did. We need to offer praise and thanksgiving as the sinful woman did, for she knew that she had sinned much and had been forgiven much. We need to adore and worship God in spirit and truth. We need to remind ourselves every day of what Jesus did for us, and then preach to our souls every day the excellent news of redemption, justification, forgiveness, sanctification, and cleansing.

We need to beseech God daily for the supernatural power to obey Him and live the Christian life. We cannot take any of the steps of WWW A MAP apart from the grace of God.

ASSIGNMENT 1: Memorize 2 Corinthians 11:3.

But I am afraid that just as Eve was deceived by the serpent's cunning, your minds may somehow be led astray from your sincere and pure devotion to Christ. —2 CORINTHIANS 11:3

- ✓ Meditate on 2 Corinthians 11:3. Jot down two or three thoughts and suggest ways to avoid being deceived.

- ✓ Write out 2 Corinthians 11:3 in your own words. Be prepared to share this with the group.

ASSIGNMENT 2: Memorize Galatians 2:20.

I have been crucified with Christ and I no longer live, but Christ lives in me. The life I now live in the body, I live by faith in the Son of God, who loved me and gave himself for me. —GALATIANS 2:20

✓ Meditate on Galatians 2:20 using the *Ask Questions* method. Jot down two or three thoughts.

✓ Write out Galatians 2:20 in your own words. Be prepared to share this with the group.

> **Ask Questions**
>
> **Is there:**
>
> A command to obey
>
> A promise to claim
>
> A sin to avoid
>
> An application to make
>
> Something new about God
>
> Ask: Who, What, When, Where, Why
>
> **Emphasize:**
> Different words
>
> **Rewrite**
> In your own words

Points to Remember

1. Jesus was the perfect sacrificial Lamb of God. The "blood" of Christ is a graphic metaphor of His sacrificial death on our behalf. God's wrath against our sin was completely satisfied through the shed blood of Jesus on the cross.

2. Because of the sacrificial death of Jesus, we have a firm standing before God. We have been forgiven, justified, sanctified, and cleansed from our sin.

3. The sacrificial death of Jesus completely paid our ransom price. We are to focus daily on Jesus, remembering the high cost of forgiveness.

✓ To summarize this lesson, write out the most important things you learned.

✓ Record how many times this week you practiced WWW A MAP: _____

✓ **Leaders**: Have the men break into pairs and practice WWW A MAP with each other. After one man works through it, have them reverse roles.

Assignment for Next Week

1. Aim to record five to seven Quiet Times this week in the following passages that speak of the sacrificial life and death of Jesus, and focus on the freedom from sin that is now ours: Galatians 5:1-14, Romans 12:1, Ephesians 4:22-24, and Ezekiel 36: 26-27.

2. Continue reviewing all the verses you've learned through this study.

3. Dedicate one Quiet Time this week to listening to or singing hymns of worship and praise to God.

4. Practice the *WAR* method of prayer in your Quiet Times this week. Focus on the worship aspect of *WAR*. Practice praying and worshiping through Psalm 103 and Romans 6. Continue praying for the men in your group to have consistent and quality times with the Lord. Pray against the Enemy's attacking the Quiet Times of the men in the group.

5. Place 2 Corinthians 11:3 in the front window of your verse pack and learn it this week. After you have memorized that verse, then place Galatians 2:20 in the verse pack window and memorize it.

6. Finish any lessons that you have not completed.

7. Be prepared to share all your Every Man A Pure Warrior verses.

8. Practice the seven critical principles for freedom—WWW A MAP— every day this week, working toward becoming a pure warrior.

9. Read through and complete next week's lesson.

PREACH THE GOSPEL TO YOURSELF DAILY

Worship

- Start worshiping God by praising Him. Sing your favorite hymn, psalm, or worship song. Offer your body and body parts to God as an act of worship and clothe your body with the armor of God.

Warfare Praying

- First, confess any known sin by praying and say the following spiritual warfare prayer. "Lord Jesus, I ask forgiveness for _____ [name any sin that comes to mind such as looking at porn, masturbation, lust, anger, unforgiveness, greed, or hate]."

- Pray the Lord's Prayer: "Our Father in heaven, hallowed be your name, your kingdom come, your will be done, on earth as it is in heaven. Give us today our daily bread, and forgive us our debts, as we also have forgiven our debtors. And lead us not into temptation, but deliver us from the evil one, for yours is the kingdom and the power and the glory forever. Amen" (Matthew 6:9-13).

- After praying the prayer, personalize it for your temptation. "Lord, please deliver me from the Tempter who is tempting me to _____. Lord, please deliver me from the Accuser who is telling me that my sin is not forgiven." If you are praying with a partner, the partner should say, "I agree in the name of Jesus."

Wounds and Triggers

- Ask the Holy Spirit to show you any wounds that are causing you to act out. Extend forgiveness to anyone who has hurt you. "Lord, I extend forgiveness to_____ for _____."

Amputate

- Separate yourself from any source of porn or lust-inducing environments. If you have just seen a pretty woman who is triggering you, begin to pray for her salvation, that she would find Christ and walk with Him.

Memorize Scripture

- Review your Scripture verses. Begin quoting out loud the verses from Psalm 103, Romans 6, EMAW verses, or any other memorized passages of Scripture.

Allies

- Call a brother for prayer when tempted, confess if you have blown it, and begin to go through these seven principles together.

Preach the Gospel to Yourself Daily

- "I thank You, Father, for the truth that 'there is now no condemnation for those who are in Christ Jesus' (Romans 8:1). I thank You, Jesus, for dying on the cross for me. I praise You that I am forgiven. You look at me as if I had never sinned, and I am adopted into Your family. You purchased me, and now I am free from sin."

LESSON 16
RADICAL TRANSFORMATION

- ✓ Have the men break into pairs and recite all their Every Man A Pure Warrior verses to each other, beginning with 2 Corinthians 11:3 and Galatians 2:20. Have one man hold the cards and say the reference while the other quotes the verse and says the reference at the end of the verse. Then have them switch roles.

- ✓ Sign off on the *Completion Records*.

- ✓ Open the session with prayer.

- ✓ Go around the room, asking each man to share one Quiet Time.

- ✓ Begin reading the lesson paragraph by paragraph.

- ✓ Have every man read his summary of how to treat a woman.

- ✓ Depending on time, have as many men as possible share their *Ask Questions*, meditations and their rewrites of Hebrews 13:4.

- ✓ Read the *Points to Remember* and the *Assignment*.

- ✓ Break into pairs and practice WWW A MAP with each other. After one man works through it, have them reverse the roles.

WWW A MAP: These Seven Fundamental Principles Must Be Mastered in the Pursuit of Purity in Our Lives. We Must Also Radically Change the Way We Perceive and Interact with Women, Especially Our Wives.

Radical Transformation: A Wife's Story

I met her after speaking at a conference she and her husband attended. She asked, "What am I supposed to do when I am never enough? I've made myself available to him sexually and purposed before God to never say no to him when he approaches me. But, because of porn, he is never satisfied. He simply wants sex all the time, two to three times a day. He keeps trying to get me to be the porn star he sees in XXX-rated videos. Because I'm not enough to satisfy him, he started visiting prostitutes. Then I got a sexually transmitted infection. One night, he woke me up because he had an erection, and demanded sex. I was in a deep sleep. I'm not saying it was rape, but it sure felt like I was just being used. I feel that most of the time. I am just being used by him."

Her husband was standing beside her as she poured out her story. He was weeping and nodding his head, full of remorse, shame, and a sense of hopelessness. He was a carnal, worldly believer, a prisoner of porn, who had brought a corrupted mind and false sexual expectations into marriage.

Sadly, I've spoken to many, many wives who have similar stories. The intimacy they looked forward to prior to marriage had been destroyed by their husbands' sexually corrupted minds and practices. Many marriages are damaged sexually because of pornography. Pornography corrupts men's minds, warps a healthy view of a woman's body, and destroys God's intent for sexuality. Pornography takes a man's normal sex drive and "supercharges" it. What God intended to be a bonding, satisfying, and exhilarating experience, shared exclusively between a man and his wife under the watchful eye of our Creator, becomes corrupted. The wife is never enough sexually. Lust is never satisfied; it always wants more.

✓ Lookup Proverbs 30:15-16. How is this man like a leech?

Another woman commented about how pornography has affected marriage. These husbands were not lovers of their wives. They were just using their wives. After intercourse, wives reported feeling used, lonely, sexually, and emotionally unsatisfied, unloved, and not connected to their husbands.

In his excellent book *The Centerfold Syndrome: How Men Can Overcome Objectification and Achieve Intimacy with Women*, psychologist Gary R. Brooks, Ph.D., identifies five principal symptoms of what he describes as a "pervasive disorder" linked to consumption of pornography.

> **Voyeurism.** An obsession with looking at women rather than interacting with them. Brooks contends that the explosion in glorification and objectification of women's bodies promotes unreal images of women, distorts physical reality, creates an obsession with visual stimulation, and trivializes all other mature features of a healthy psychosexual relationship.

✓ Lookup Judges 14:2,3. How did Samson demonstrate voyeurism?

> **Objectification.** An attitude in which women are objects rated by size, shape, and harmony of body parts. Brooks asserts that if a man spends most of his emotional energy on sexual fantasies about inaccessible people, he frequently will not be available for even the most intimate emotional and sexual moments with his partner.
>
> **Validation.** The need to validate masculinity through beautiful women. According to Brooks, the women who meet centerfold standards only retain their power as long as they maintain perfect bodies and the leverage of mystery and unavailability. And, the great majority of men who never come close to sex with their dream woman are left feeling cheated or unmanly.

✓ Lookup 1 Samuel 25:2-3, 39, and 2 Samuel 11:2-4.

✓ How did King David model this principle?

Trophyism. The idea that beautiful women are collectibles who show the world who a man is. Brooks asserts that the women's-bodies-as-trophies mentality, damaging enough in adolescence, becomes even more destructive in adulthood. Furthermore, trophies, once they are won, are supposed to become the property of the winner, a permanent physical symbol of accomplishment and worthiness. This cannot be so with women's bodies.

✓ Lookup Esther 1:10-11. How did the king demonstrate trophyism?

Fear of true intimacy. Inability to relate to women honestly and intimately despite deep loneliness. Pornography pays scant attention to men's needs for sensuality and intimacy while exalting their sexual needs. Thus some men develop a preoccupation with sexuality, which powerfully handicaps their capacity for emotionally intimate relationships with men and for nonsexual relationships with women.

✓ Which consequences of looking at porn did the husband in the wife's story suffer from?

✓ How did these affect his marriage relationship?

From "Sex Objects" to "Fellow Kingdom Warriors"

Carolyn Custis James wrote a marvelous book called, *Half the Church; Recapturing God's Global Vision for Women*. The following excerpts provide a view of women that is vastly different from the one provided through porn.

> God created the man out of earth and placed him in the garden. Then suddenly and rather dramatically, for the first time in the creation narrative, God is not pleased. There's a problem in Eden, and God both names and solves it. *"It is not good for the man to be alone. I will make an **ezer kenegdo** for him..."*
>
> God could easily have taken another fistful of earth to create the woman. Instead, He creates the *ezer* from Adam's body—by taking "a rib" from Adam while he was in a deep sleep...
>
> **The whole human race, beginning with Eve, comes from Adam's wounded side....**
> She will be his strongest ally in pursuing God's purposes and his first roadblock when he veers off course. Long before I started digging, scholars tallied up the twenty-one times *ezer* appears in the Old Testament: twice in Genesis for the woman (Genesis 2:18, 20), three times for nations to whom Israel appealed for military aid (Isaiah 30:5, Ezekiel 12:14, Daniel 11:34), and here's the kicker—sixteen times for God as Israel's helper

(Exodus 18:4; Deuteronomy 33:7, 26, 29; Psalm 20:2; 33:20; 70:5; 89:19 [translated "strength" in the NIV]; 115:9, 10, 11; 121:1-2; 124:8; 146:5; and Hosea 13:9).

✓ Lookup some of the following verses, which are mentioned above. Note the context of how God described Himself as Israel's *ezer*.

Exodus 18:4

Deuteronomy 33:7, 26, 29

Psalm 20:2

Psalm 33:20

Again, quoting from *Half the Church*:

> I read all those verses and discovered *ezer* is used consistently in a military context. Israel seeks military aid from her neighbors. God is his people's "shield and defense," "better than chariots and horses," standing "sentry watch over his people."
>
> Remarkably, even Eden fits this pattern, for although some may balk at the thought, it is fair to say that even the idyllic garden of Eden was a war zone. The command to rule and subdue put God's image-bearers on high alert, that fierce resistance lay ahead. God commanded the man to keep, or guard, the garden by using the same military language later used for the cherubim who guarded the garden with a flaming sword—a primeval light saber—after Adam and Eve are evicted (Genesis 3:24). The reason, of course, is that a powerful Enemy is already plotting an attack.
>
> Putting the facts together, isn't it obvious that the *ezer* is a warrior? In addition, don't we already know this in our bones? God created his daughters to be ezer–warriors with our brothers. He deploys the *ezer* to break the man's aloneness by soldiering

with him wholeheartedly and at full strength for God's gracious kingdom. The man needs everything she brings to their global mission. Other factors confirmed my conclusions. Of course, the strength God brings as *ezer* to his people should be sufficient to convince us that as *ezers* one must be strong, resourceful, and alert to the cries of the needy and oppressed, and proactive, too.

Support for the *ezer*-warrior comes from other Bible passages that use military language for women. Both Ruth and the Proverbs 31 woman are called women of valor (*hayil*). Paul rallies believers, both men and women, to "put on all of God's armor" (Ephesians 6: 10-17) in preparation to do battle with the Evil One, reminding us that our battle is "not ... against flesh-and-blood enemies" (Ephesians 6:12). Thinking of the *ezer* as a warrior is entirely consistent with how Scripture views us. This changes everything for women and girls! God deploys his daughters—all of us—to be *ezer*-warriors for his kingdom all the days of our lives.

✓ Write three or four observations from these paragraphs.

✓ How does porn's view of women compare with God's purposes for women—calling them *ezer kenegdo*, strong warrior-helpers to advance His kingdom?

✓ The following passages give God's commands and expectations for sex in marriage. Read them with a view of how pornography affects how a man sexually treats his bride.

Read Matthew 5:27-28. What is the result of looking lustfully at women?

Read Hebrews 13:4. What happens to those who don't honor marriage and allow sex to be defiled?

Read 1 Corinthians 7:1-5. Who should have control over your body? Who should cause your erections, your wife, or a porn star?

1 Thessalonians 4:3-8 *"For God wants you to be holy and pure and to keep clear of all sexual sin so that each of you will marry in holiness and honor—not in lustful passion as the heathen do, in their ignorance of God and his ways. And this also is God's will: that you never cheat in this matter by taking another man's wife because the Lord will punish you terribly for this, as we have solemnly told you before. For God has not called us to be dirty-minded and full of lust but to be holy and clean. If anyone refuses to live by these rules, he is not disobeying the rules of men but of God who gives his Holy Spirit to you"* (Living Bible).

✓ What principles for how to treat a woman are found in the preceding passage?

✓ 1 Thessalonians 4:5 says, *"not in lustful passion as the heathen do."* (TLB) List what 1 Peter 4:2-5 says the differences are between how a believer should treat a woman, and how a nonbeliever treats a woman?

✓ Read 1 Corinthians 13:4-7 and 1 Corinthians 7:1-5.
How is the teaching of *"love does not insist on its own way"* (1 Corinthians 13:5 RSV) compatible with the teaching that *"because of the temptation for immorality, each man should have his own wife"* (1 Corinthians 7:2 RSV)? How should a man handle his sex drive when his wife is unavailable or not interested?

Job was married, yet he said, *"I made a covenant with my eyes not to look lustfully at a young woman"* (Job 31:1). In Mark 7:20-23 Jesus said, *"From within, out of the heart of men, proceed evil thoughts, adulteries, fornications, murders, thefts, covetousness, wickedness, deceit, lewdness, an evil eye, blasphemy, pride, and foolishness. All these evil things come from within and defile a man."* If you look lustfully at a woman and then fantasize in your heart that your wife is that young woman while you have sex, who are you really having sex with?

My enslavement to pornography almost destroyed my marriage. When I started applying the principles of WWW A MAP and growing toward purity and wholeness, God revealed to me a number of lies that I had believed, and convicted me of believing them. I had seen my wife primarily as a sex object. When I would look at her, it was with lust, not with love. I approached sex as a right and demanded it. I put my sexual urges above her well-being. It's not something I am proud of. I had drunk the full measure of the lies of pornography.

✓ Lookup Psalm 139:23-24. Ask the Holy Spirit to search your heart in this area of sexual conduct in marriage. Ask yourself, "Have I treated my wife in honor as a man of God or like a nonbeliever who doesn't know God? Have I brought the lies of pornography into my marriage bed? Have I truly loved my wife in the spirit of 1 Corinthians 13:4-7?" Record what the Holy Spirit reveals to you.

✓ If you feel that you have dishonored your wife, I challenge you to seek God's face and ask for the grace to repent, and to apologize to your wife for failing to love her honorably. Outline the specific steps you need to take to apologize.

James 5:16 says, "... *confess your sins to one another and pray for one another that you may be healed*" (ESV). I felt led by God to confess my sexual sins to my wife, that I had dishonored her, and used her. I felt led by God to ask her for forgiveness for wronging her and for being sexually selfish. I needed to confess that I had ruined our relationship sexually and placed our marriage in jeopardy.

First Thessalonians 4:3-8, says, in effect, that we are not to take our wives sexually in the passion of lust, like heathen who do not know God, and that no one should defraud his brother (wife) in this manner for God is an avenger in all these things.

Confessing was *extremely hard* to do. Like anything God calls us to do, it takes His grace and power to obey. I cried out to God, claiming Hebrews 4:15-16: "*We do not have a high priest who is unable to empathize with our weaknesses, but we have one who has been tempted in every way, just as we are—yet he did not sin. Let us then approach God's throne of grace with confidence, so that we may receive mercy and find grace to help us in our time of need.*"

I asked my wife for forgiveness and asked if we could restart our sexual relationship. God gave her the grace to forgive me and to begin our relationship anew.

If your wife suffers from chronic depression, has been raped or abused, or has suicidal tendencies, it might be wise to not share these things with her. Ephesians 4:29 applies: **"Do not let any unwholesome talk come out of your mouths, but only what is helpful for building others up according to their needs, that it may benefit those who listen."**

✓ Write a summary of what you have learned in this lesson about how to treat a woman. Be prepared to share it with the group.

ASSIGNMENT: Memorize Hebrews 13:4.

Marriage should be honored by all, and the marriage bed kept pure, for God will judge the adulterer and all the sexually immoral.
—HEBREWS 13:4

✓ Meditate on Hebrews 13:4, using the Ask Questions method. Jot down two or three thoughts.

Ask Questions

Is there:

A command to obey

A promise to claim

A sin to avoid

An application to make

Something new about God

Ask: Who, What, When, Where, Why

Emphasize:
Different words

Rewrite
In your own words

✓ Write out Hebrews 13:4 in your own words. Be prepared to share this with the group.

Points to Remember

1. Pornography poisons our souls, affecting how we relate to the opposite sex. Porn reduces a woman's value to a single dimension, her sexiness.

2. Pornography corrupts a man's mind and warps his expectations for intimacy in marriage. Men exposed to pornography bring pagan, worldly attitudes to the marriage bed, defiling it by dishonoring their wives.

3. God commands us to treat our wives in purity and, not in the *"... passion of lust like heathen who do not know God"* (1 Thessalonians 4:5 RSV). We must honor and love them as our marriage vows dictate.

4. Your wife was created to be a suitable helper for you, worth forsaking all others for. Her worth is far above jewels.

✓ To summarize this lesson, write out the most important things you learned.

RADICAL TRANSFORMATION

✓ Record how many times this week you practiced WWW A MAP:
_____

✓ **Leaders**: Have the men break into pairs and practice WWW A MAP with each other. After one man works through it, have them reverse roles.

EVERY MAN A WARRIOR

ASSIGNMENT FOR NEXT WEEK

1. Aim to record five to seven Quiet Times this week in the passages that focus on the freedom from sin that is now ours because of Jesus' blood. Have your Quiet Times this week in Romans 6, 7, and 8.

2. Continue reviewing all the verses you've learned through this study.

3. Dedicate one Quiet Time this week to listening to or singing hymns of worship and praise to God.

4. Practice the *WAR* method of prayer in your Quiet Times this week. Focus on the worship aspect of *WAR*. Practice praying and worshiping through Psalm 103 and Romans 6. Continue praying for the men in your group to have consistent and quality times with the Lord. Pray against the Enemy's attacking the Quiet Times of the men in the group.

5. Place Hebrews 13:4 in the front window of your verse pack and learn it this week.

6. Finish any lessons that you have not completed.

7. Be prepared to share all your Every Man A Pure Warrior verses.

8. Practice the seven critical principles for freedom—WWW A MAP—every day this week, working toward becoming a pure warrior.

9. Read through and complete next week's lesson.

WWW A MAP — Seven Keys to Freedom

Worship
- Start worshiping God by praising Him. Sing your favorite hymn, psalm, or worship song. Offer your body and body parts to God as an act of worship and clothe your body with the armor of God.

Warfare Praying
- First, confess any known sin by praying and say the following spiritual warfare prayer. "Lord Jesus, I ask forgiveness for _____ [name any sin that comes to mind such as looking at porn, masturbation, lust, anger, unforgiveness, greed, or hate]."
- Pray the Lord's Prayer: "Our Father in heaven, hallowed be your name, your kingdom come, your will be done, on earth as it is in heaven. Give us today our daily bread, and forgive us our debts, as we also have forgiven our debtors. And lead us not into temptation, but deliver us from the evil one, for yours is the kingdom and the power and the glory forever. Amen" (Matthew 6:9-13).
- After praying the prayer, personalize it for your temptation. "Lord, please deliver me from the Tempter who is tempting me to _____. Lord, please deliver me from the Accuser who is telling me that my sin is not forgiven." If you are praying with a partner, the partner should say, "I agree in the name of Jesus."

Wounds and Triggers
- Ask the Holy Spirit to show you any wounds that are causing you to act out. Extend forgiveness to anyone who has hurt you. "Lord, I extend forgiveness to_____ for _____."

Amputate
- Separate yourself from any source of porn or lust-inducing environments. If you have just seen a pretty woman who is triggering you, begin to pray for her salvation, that she would find Christ and walk with Him.

Memorize Scripture
- Review your Scripture verses. Begin quoting out loud the verses from Psalm 103, Romans 6, EMAW verses, or any other memorized passages of Scripture.

Allies
- Call a brother for prayer when tempted, confess if you have blown it, and begin to go through these seven principles together.

Preach the Gospel to Yourself Daily
- "I thank You, Father, for the truth that 'there is now no condemnation for those who are in Christ Jesus' (Romans 8:1). I thank You, Jesus, for dying on the cross for me. I praise You that I am forgiven. You look at me as if I had never sinned, and I am adopted into Your family. You purchased me, and now I am free from sin."

LESSON 17
HOPE: REVIEW AND APPLY

✓ Have the men break into pairs and recite all their Every Man A Pure Warrior verses to each other, beginning with Hebrews 13:4. Have one man hold the cards and say the reference while the other quotes the verse and says the reference at the end of the verse. Then have them switch roles.

✓ Count how many times you have practiced WWW A MAP since lesson 11.

✓ Sign off on the *Completion Records*.

✓ Open the session with prayer.

✓ Go around the room, asking each man to share one Quiet Time.

✓ Begin reading the lesson paragraph by paragraph.

✓ Depending on time, have as many men as possible share their *Ask Questions*, meditations and their rewrites of 2 Peter 1:3-4.

✓ Break into pairs and practice WWW A MAP with each other. After one man works through it, have them reverse the roles.

✓ Read the *Points to Remember* and the *Assignment for Life*.

✓ Suggest you plan a graduation dinner for those who have successfully completed *Every Man A Pure Warrior*. Please go to: www.everymanapurewarrior.com to download a Certificate of Completion.

In Conclusion, the WWW A MAP Fundamental Principles Need to Be Mastered in the Pursuit of Purity in Our Own Lives and As We Seek to Help Others Who Are Struggling with Lust and Porn.

From Hopeless Despair to Restoration

Andre was referred to me by a friend. We soon met at a local coffee shop, where Andre poured out his story. Over the next ninety minutes, he never stopped weeping; tears were streaming down his face. His wife of twelve years was leaving him. Her parents were driving fifteen hundred miles to take their daughter and the four young children away from Andre.

A week prior to that, Andre's wife was diagnosed with a sexually transmitted disease. She knew she had been faithful to her wedding vows, so she had to have been infected by her husband. When she confronted Andre, he confessed that he had been visiting prostitutes. She immediately kicked him out of the house. It was not the first time he had been unfaithful. She had forgiven him before, but this was the last straw!

I asked Andre to tell me his sexual history. He had grown up in a dysfunctional home, where pornography was readily available. His first exposure to porn was at age six. He was hooked and watched it every chance he could. By the age of nine, he was playing touchy-feely with neighbor girls, and at age eleven he lost his virginity. All through his high school and college years, he spent hours every day consuming porn, masturbating, or fornicating.

Even after he became a believer, he had maintained a secret, double life. He had tried and failed many, many times to stop his immoral lifestyle, but always fell back into the habits that he had developed as a young, pre-adolescent male. No one had helped him in his struggles. Andre had no practical tools to use in the fight for purity. He was convinced that once he married, his lust problems would be solved. After marriage, he slowly resumed looking at porn again, and then the babies came, and his dear wife was less available and less interested in sex. He started cruising for sexual release outside of marriage. First, it was back to porn, then strip clubs, and then—as sin always progresses—he hired his first prostitute. Later, it became easier to visit sex workers than to do the hard work of cultivating a healthy relationship with his wife and exercising sexual self-control.

Now he was losing it all: his marriage, his kids, his reputation, and possibly his job. He was distraught, lonely, broken, and hopeless. When he was done telling me his sexual history, he asked if there was anything I could do to help him. My heart had been breaking as I listened to him. I replied, "Yes, yes, yes, there is hope for you. Your life is *not* over, but if you really want to be changed, to be transformed, it will take work on your part." I thought of the seven principles in WWW A MAP. *Which one do I talk about first? How do I explain these principles to him without overwhelming him?*

- ✓ Lookup 2 Peter 1:3-4 and Philippians 2:12-16. According to these passages, what is the basis of hope?

With Andre, the first principle that I started with was **Allies**. I affirmed his decision to seek me out. I asked him if he wanted to meet frequently and regularly for encouragement in the battle for purity. He eagerly agreed and rearranged his schedule so we could meet. He was enlisting me as an ally in this struggle. We continued meeting several times each week, for several hours each time, until he moved out of the area.

- ✓ **Allies.** Review lesson 3. Summarize the necessity of having brothers in the battle. Describe how you found your ally and how he helped you battle against porn. List some characteristics of a successful ally.

I wanted to give him something positive to do right away. The next two principles that I explained were to memorize verses of Scripture and to preach the gospel to himself daily. I challenged Andre to immediately start memorizing twenty-three verses of Scripture. I told him, "I know it seems like a lot, but you can do this. You are spending hours each day fulfilling your lusts. Are you willing to spend two hours a day reading and rereading the same passage, over and over again, until you have memorized it perfectly?" He said he would try.

The passage that I chose was Romans 6. This is the best chapter in the Scriptures that speaks of our freedom from sin because of Christ's death, burial, and resurrection.

Andre was experiencing the death of his marriage, death of his fatherhood, death of his reputation, and death of hope, all because of his enslavement to lust. By memorizing this chapter in Romans, Andre would be rebuilding his mind with the spiritual, life-giving truths of the gospel. By reviewing the passage hundreds of times, he would be preaching the gospel to himself daily.

- ✓ **Memorize and Meditate on Scripture.** Review lesson 4. Write at least three key points summarizing some of the main reasons why memorizing and meditating on Scripture is a key to becoming pure. Ask the Holy Spirit for a lifetime goal for Scripture memory. Be prepared to share your paragraphs and goal with your group.

- ✓ **Preach the gospel to yourself daily**. Review lesson 15. Summarize the aspects of the gospel that most impact you and help you in the area of purity. *Tell how the Gospel is both good and bad news.*

Andre took up the challenge and started memorizing Romans 6. Every time he was tempted, he would quote out loud Romans 6. He replaced the word *sin* with *lust*, *porn*, and *masturbation*. His mind was directed toward Christ. He immediately started experiencing victory. Before our initial meeting, he was hopeless and despairing of life itself. Now, within a week, he had hope and was experiencing freedom for the first time in decades.

At our second meeting, I challenged him to rid his environment of all things that would stir up lust. I exhorted him to destroy all his porn, all access to porn, and to install porn-blocking filters on all his electronic devices.

- ✓ **Amputate and Blockade.** Review lesson 14. Write several paragraphs summarizing what you have learned about creating a safe environment where you live, work, and play. Tell your group what you have amputated (removed from your life) and how you have blocked exposure to porn in your quest to get and stay pure. Reveal to the men what other things need to be amputated and/or blocked.

Andre was still under a cloud of shame, guilt, and condemnation. He was being tempted numerous times throughout the day. The next principle that we discussed was spiritual warfare. This was a new thought for him. He understood the principles and memorized the *Lord's Prayer* and started practicing this discipline. The next time I saw Andre, his whole countenance had changed. For the first time since I met him, he was smiling, and believing that long-term victory was possible.

✓ **Warfare**. Review lessons 8, 9 and 10. Write at least three key points summarizing what you have learned about spiritual warfare and purity. Ask the Lord to show you insights into what needs to change in your spiritual life in this area. Be prepared to share your insights with your group.

It was only natural for Andre to want to express praise and worship to God. He was experiencing freedom. He was tasting the joy of a clear conscience and was daring to believe that God loved him. The clouds of darkness and shame were gone. He was growing in his dependence on Jesus and believing the gospel.

I shared with Andre the next principle: worship. I challenged him to memorize another passage of Scripture, Psalm 103. I wanted him to meet every temptation with praise and worship. He had already mastered Romans 6, so I knew that with diligence and discipline, he would add this psalm to his arsenal. I taught Andre the power of praise through song. We then went over the daily offering up of his body and body parts to God and how, through prayer, to put on God's armor.

✓ **Worship**. Review lessons 5, 6, and 7. Summarize what you have learned about the connection between worship and purity. Write down what the Holy Spirit is asking you to do to become a better worshiper. Be prepared to share with your group.

In our next session, Andre and I discussed wounds and triggers. As with so many other men, Andre's family life when he was a child was less than ideal. There were dysfunctional parenting and easy access to porn. He was filled with resentment and hatred toward his parents for the wounds they had caused. We went through the process of healing wounds found in lessons 11, 12, and 13.

✓ **Wounds and Triggers**. Review lessons 11, 12, and 13. Summarize any connection in your life between wounds and purity. Be prepared to explain to your group what specific action you are taking or will take to receive healing.

After three months of separation, Andre went to see his wife and children. When she saw her husband, she recognized that he was broken and repentant. Moreover, he now had hope and had been walking in purity for three months. The Holy Spirit prompted her to forgive him and restart their relationship. They are now living together again as husband and wife. His marriage, once dead, is now very much alive. His hopes of being a responsible and godly father are more likely to happen.

Victory over porn is possible! Victory over *any* sin is possible through the indwelling presence of God, the lavish gifts of His grace, and the power of the Word. Praise God for the promises that through Christ, He has given us *everything we need for life and godliness.*

ASSIGNMENT: Memorize 2 Peter 1:3-4.

His divine power has given us everything we need for a godly life through our knowledge of him who called us by his own glory and goodness. Through these he has given us his very great and precious promises, so that through them you may participate in the divine nature, having escaped the corruption in the world caused by evil desires. —2 Peter 1:3-4

✓ Meditate on 2 Peter 1:3-4, using the Ask Questions method. Jot down two or three thoughts.

> **Ask Questions**
>
> **Is there:**
>
> A command to obey
>
> A promise to claim
>
> A sin to avoid
>
> An application to make
>
> Something new about God
>
> Ask: Who, What, When, Where, Why
>
> **Emphasize:**
> Different words
>
> **Rewrite**
> In your own words

✓ Rewrite 2 Peter 1:3-4 in your own words. Be prepared to share this with the group.

✓ Read the *Assignment for Life* on page 202, and list the things that you believe God would have you to do. Be prepared to share your plans with your group.

✓ Review your Completion Record. Be prepared to discuss with your group what you still need to do to successfully complete the requirements of Every Man A Pure Warrior.

Points to Remember

1. Purity is possible. God *has* given to us everything we need to live a godly life!

2. There are seven fundamental principles that we must know, understand, and apply in our quest to get and to stay pure and to escape the snare of pornography: WWW A MAP.

3. God is in the business of giving new life. He who raises the dead can give life to our dead, lust-filled bodies also.

✓ Record how many times you practiced WWW A MAP over the last 6 weeks: _____

✓ Have the men break into pairs and practice WWW A MAP with each other. After one man works through it, have them reverse roles.

Assignment for Life

1. Continue to have consistent Quiet Times. Journal your thoughts when possible.

2. In the appendix, you'll find a list of additional verses to memorize and meditate on. Make it a lifetime goal to continue memorizing verses. Seek to add at least one verse each week until you die. We can never learn too many verses. As you learn more and more verses, you'll need to spend more time reviewing than memorizing new verses. Keep reviewing and asking God to reveal truth to you as you meditate.

3. Keep practicing the *WAR* (Worship, Admit, Request) method of prayer in your Quiet Times (from EMAW Book 1, Lesson 7). Begin praying for the men in your group and other men whom the Lord brings into your life. Pray that they would have consistent and quality times with the Lord. Pray against the Enemy attacking the Quiet Times of the men in your sphere of influence.

4. Place 2 Peter 1:3-4 in the front window of your verse pack and memorize it this week.

5. Finish any lessons that you have not completed.

6. Practice WWW A MAP every day and every time you are tempted sexually. Remember this: if you fall or stumble, it is grievous, but you are normal. Obey with determination Proverbs 24:16 *"... a righteous man falls seven times, **and rises again** ..."* (RSV, emphasis mine).

7. Seek to continue learning and becoming a master at spiritual warfare. Never stop reading and learning.

8. Continue to develop allies in the ongoing battle for purity. None of us will make it or finish well by being alone. God always intended for us to be connected with others in community, and He commands us to do so. Continue to meet with your allies to grow and to encourage each other in having Quiet Times and in the ongoing discipline of Scripture memory and meditation.

9. Join with other men and teenage boys in building up the next generation of men who will fight to be pure and to create an environment in which women are honored and not abused.

10. After successfully completing this course, you now have the knowledge and the tools to help other men escape from the pit of porn. Purity is possible! Hopefully, as you continue your own battle to keep pure, pray that God will give you other men in which to invest. Ask God for a group of men that you can lead through the four books of the EMAW series. Implant into these men the vision to reach out to other men so that these spiritual principles will continue to be shared.

11. There are other lessons written on sexual purity that are available on the *Every Man A Pure Warrior* website (everymanapurewarrior.com). Other resources can be found there as well. Use these lessons and resources as you lead and disciple men.

12. Seek to become not just a worshiper of God but a great worshiper of God. Psalm 145:3 says, *"Great is the LORD and greatly to be praised, and his greatness is unsearchable"* (RSV). God is a great God who deserves great praise!

WWW A MAP: Seven Keys to Freedom

Worship

- Start worshiping God by praising Him. Sing your favorite hymn, psalm, or worship song. Offer your body and body parts to God as an act of worship and clothe your body with the armor of God.

Warfare Praying

- First, confess any known sin by praying and say the following spiritual warfare prayer. "Lord Jesus, I ask forgiveness for _____ [name any sin that comes to mind such as looking at porn, masturbation, lust, anger, unforgiveness, greed, or hate]."

- Pray the Lord's Prayer: "Our Father in heaven, hallowed be your name, your kingdom come, your will be done, on earth as it is in heaven. Give us today our daily bread, and forgive us our debts, as we also have forgiven our debtors. And lead us not into temptation, but deliver us from the evil one, for yours is the kingdom and the power and the glory forever. Amen" (Matthew 6:9-13).

- After praying the prayer, personalize it for your temptation. "Lord, please deliver me from the Tempter who is tempting me to _____. Lord, please deliver me from the Accuser who is telling me that my sin is not forgiven." If you are praying with a partner, the partner should say, "I agree in the name of Jesus."

Wounds and Triggers

- Ask the Holy Spirit to show you any wounds that are causing you to act out. Extend forgiveness to anyone who has hurt you. "Lord, I extend forgiveness to_____ for _____."

Amputate

- Separate yourself from any source of porn or lust-inducing environments. If you have just seen a pretty woman who is triggering you, begin to pray for her salvation, that she would find Christ and walk with Him.

Memorize Scripture

- Review your Scripture verses. Begin quoting out loud the verses from Psalm 103, Romans 6, EMAW verses, or any other memorized passages of Scripture.

Allies

- Call a brother for prayer when tempted, confess if you have blown it, and begin to go through these seven principles together.

Preach the Gospel to Yourself Daily

- "I thank You, Father, for the truth that 'there is now no condemnation for those who are in Christ Jesus' (Romans 8:1). I thank You, Jesus, for dying on the cross for me. I praise You that I am forgiven. You look at me as if I had never sinned, and I am adopted into Your family. You purchased me, and now I am free from sin."

Appendix

Note to Leaders

Biblical Foundations for Spiritual Warfare Prayer

The Every Man A Warrior Icon

Emotional Pain Words

Quiet Time Journal

Completion Record

Purity Pack NIV Verses

Making a Difference

About the Author

Note to Leaders

Thank you for agreeing to serve as a leader of an *Every Man A Pure Warrior* group. Your role is critical to ensuring the success of the course.

This curriculum may be the most sensitive and hardest of any you will ever encounter. Pornography has swept over civilization like a tsunami. Almost every man, woman and child has been or will be impacted by the disastrous lies of porn and sexual sin.

How you lead your group, and the atmosphere you create in your group will either open doors for men to share the deep hurts and wounds of their lives, or shut the door for these men to share. Here are some things to pray through and think about.

- You as the leader set the degree of vulnerability for the men in your group. If you are open and honest and share the dark parts of your soul, then men in your group will feel more comfortable in sharing their brokenness. If you hide and are not open, your men will also tend to hide.

- If you act shocked or disgusted or condemn men with either your voice or body language when they share their histories or struggles, men in pain will immediately sense that you are unsafe and will shut down.

- Set the pace in being open and vulnerable by going *first*. This gives the men the gift of going second.

We have developed a course that we believe will give men the keys to freedom. Our prayer and assertion are that each man's quest for purity will be significantly enhanced and improved by this curriculum.

- The next points will be hard to read and are meant not to scare you off, but to prepare you for worst-case scenarios.

- All people sin. Unfortunately, in the realm of sexual sin, not all sins are created equal. Society accepts the viewing of porn. If a man looks at porn regularly in the privacy of his home, then masturbates privately and alone, no one thinks this unusual or even wrong. However, for a man who wants to please God and grow in holiness, these actions are understood differently.

- Sin is never stagnant. Romans 6:19 says, *"Just as you once yielded your members to impurity and to greater and greater iniquity..."* (RSV). James 1:15 says, *"Desire, when it is conceived gives birth to sin and sin when it is full grown brings forth death"* (RSV).
- There is a logical continuum and many manifestations of sexual sin.
    - *Exposure to porn, normally one man, one woman.*
    - *Leading to heterosexual promiscuity and if married to adultery.*
    - *Watching porn progresses to one man, two women.*
    - *Then porn progresses to watching lesbian sex.*
    - *Then porn progresses to watching orgies.*
    - *Then porn progresses to gay sex.*
    - *Then porn progresses to BDSM, bestiality.*
    - *Then porn progresses to rape fantasies.*
    - *Then porn progresses to child porn.*
    - *At some point, satisfaction with porn diminishes and porn doesn't satisfy anymore.*
    - *Sex partners are sought out: prostitutes, morally loose partners, massage sex, bisexualism, homosexuality, etc.*
    - *Depending on psychosexual imprinting, a person could move toward flashing or voyeurism.*
    - *Sexual norms are compromised: could move into assaults, rapes, etc.*
    - *Normal sexual activities are thwarted, leading to attempts to have sex with younger and younger partners, sex with minors, etc.*
- For some, sin may have progressed to where it is no longer simply a sin. Society determines which sins move to the criminal level.
- If a man progresses in his sin to become a peeping Tom or a flasher or assaults, molests, or rapes someone or moves into possessing child porn or acts out by soliciting prostitutes or solicits or has contact with a minor with the intent of sexual contact, these acts are considered crimes. As such, some of these acts are considered serious crimes, and there are laws requiring mandatory reporting. Each state has different laws and statutes of limitations regarding mandatory reporting.

- Here is a partial list of mandatory reporters. Each state and country may differ.
  - *child-care providers*
  - *caregivers*
  - *clergy (clergy-penitent privileged communication is exempt in most states) counselors and other mental health professionals*
  - *medical examiners and coroners*
  - *health care providers*
  - *police and other law enforcement officers*
  - *schoolteachers, coaches, guidance counselors, principals and other school personnel*
  - *social workers*
  - *women's health clinic practitioners (in some states)*
  - *film developers (for child pornography purposes)*
- If a man confesses in your group some sin or crime that requires mandatory reporting, you will now be faced with some difficult decisions. If you are an ordained pastor or a licensed counselor or a church staff member or one of these mandatory reporters, you are required ethically and morally to protect the flock and report the crime.
- Yet we don't want to abandon a broken man who is repentant and trapped and wants help. You must encourage the man to go to the proper authorities and make a full confession. If in the rare case when a man's sin has progressed into the realm of the criminal, I would encourage you to go with the man as he turns himself in. The civil authorities may press charges and your man may face jail time or probation and/or may be forced to register as a sex offender. In all this, God promises to never leave us or forsake us, and the man needs brothers around to support and encourage and love him through the process. There is no sin that can't be forgiven and no habits that can't be changed. God is in the transformation business.
- As a leader, awareness of legal implications is not to scare you, but to prepare you to lead a group.

- Jesus' mission was to set the captives free, to heal the brokenhearted, to bind up wounds. Our desire is to help all men who are broken, captive, and wounded, and to address sexual sin long before it has progressed to the criminal level.
- *Every Man A Pure Warrior* will help any person who is caught up in the porn cycle, regardless of where they are on the continuum of sexual sin.
- *Every Man A Pure Warrior* is not intended as a professional counseling course. I am not a professional counselor. I am an ordained minister and a professional disciplemaker. All lessons in this book are written with transformation in mind, to set free captives of sexual sin. If at any time you feel that you are over your head, please refer members of your group to a professional, licensed counselor.
- For a few men, the depth of shame is so great that they may indicate a desire for self-harm. If at any time you sense that a man in the midst of battling for purity has lost hope and is full of despair, and he speaks or implies suicidal thoughts, immediately refer this dear brother to professional counselors.

BIBLICAL FOUNDATIONS FOR SPIRITUAL WARFARE PRAYER

Foreword by Bob Reehm

The following teaching was written by Lonnie Berger, author of Every Man A Warrior. It is about a more advanced form of spiritual warfare praying. The scriptural basis for warfare praying is explained in this appendix.

I have found this kind of prayer to be very effective in my own life and in the lives of many of the men that I've discipled. I would encourage you to be like a Berean Christian. In Acts 17:11 the Bereans searched out the Scriptures to see if the things that Paul was teaching them were accurate or not. Study this appendix and make your own conclusions about warfare prayer.

When I was assigned to pioneer a ministry on a military base in California, I did all the things that I had been taught to successfully start a ministry. I did evangelism, challenged men toward discipleship, conducted spiritual interest surveys, recruited a prayer team, and so forth, but all these efforts yielded NO spiritual fruit. No one came to Christ.

After working diligently at this for several months, I had an hour-long complaint session with God. Listening to me whine and moan, the Holy Spirit gently brought to mind the teaching of Jesus in Mark 3:27 which says that *"no one can enter a strong man's house and plunder his goods, unless he first binds the strong man"* (ESV). And then it struck me that I had not yet bound the strong man! I read the passage again and it became very clear that what I needed to do was warfare praying.

Empowered by this counsel, I did a prayer walk around the barracks, claiming the area for Jesus. I specifically prayed, asking the Lord to bind the deceiving spirits and every demon of doubt, of unbelief, or of hard hearts, that were keeping young military personnel locked in darkness. After walking around the barracks seven times, praying for fruit and binding the strong man I felt a spiritual breakthrough. Within a week, God brought fruit! One man came to Christ and a Bible study started in the barracks which led to numerous men being discipled.

Paul teaches in Ephesians 6:12 that our fight is not with people but against spiritual forces of evil. In places of great darkness, the Evil One must be subdued before new fruit can be born.

If you are under demonic attack, feel you are hitting a brick wall in personal character growth, or your ministry advances have stalled, I encourage you to read carefully Lonnie Berger's teaching, below, and experiment with this kind of praying. We must bind the strongman. I was set free from a forty-year addiction to porn and have seen many men get spiritual breakthroughs in their battle for purity by praying this kind of spiritual warfare prayer.

Biblical Foundations for Spiritual Warfare Prayer by Lonnie Berger, founder of Every Man A Warrior

In 1975, I came to Christ and immediately had a hunger for the Word. In reading the Scripture, I came across a passage where Jesus cast out demons, and as a new believer, I was intrigued as to what this meant. The next Sunday, my pastor spoke on this issue and assured the congregation that since the United States was a Christian nation that meant demonic activity was rare, only happening in places like Africa, and therefore should be ignored. I remained ignorant on this subject for the next fifteen years.

In the early 1990s, my family encountered serious spiritual attacks. My children, age three and five, were harassed each night by demonic dreams and would wake up screaming and describing the ugly creatures that were trying to bite them. After seeing my own children under such oppressive assaults, my theology of "demons only happen in Africa" went out the window.

I began to ask God for help and was led to Dr. Charles Kraft at Fuller Theological Seminary to get training in spiritual warfare. Dr. Kraft is a conservative theologian, graduated from Wheaton College, Ashland Theological Seminary and served as a missionary in Nigeria during the 1950s.

Dr. Kraft has written several books on this subject. His material was instrumental in helping to lay a biblical foundation for how I would understand spiritual warfare. Over the years, I have used these principles to help many people find freedom from spiritual oppression.

The Spiritual Warfare Prayer

In the name of Jesus, I bind every demon that has an assignment against me. I cancel your assignments, I cut you off from your spiritual head, I break any curses that give you strength, and I command all of you to be bound together and cast into the abyss. Be gone in the name of Jesus. Do not return, do not send replacements. I command this in Jesus' name.

Biblical Foundations for Spiritual Warfare Prayer

- Jesus often dealt with demons but was never afraid of them or tried to deny their existence. Nearly half of the chapters of Mark and one-third of the chapters in the Gospels of Matthew and Luke reveal a story of a demonic encounter.
- Jesus gave his disciples *"authority to drive out demons"* as part of normal ministry (Luke 9:1-2).

- His disciples, both the twelve and the seventy-two, used this authority with success and were joyful that they could set people free (Luke 10:17-19).
- Jesus gave specific commands to the demons and spoke directly to them. In Luke 4:35 Jesus used the command to: *"be quiet"*, and *"come out of him!"*
- After Jesus' resurrection, the disciples in the book of Acts continued to cast out demons as a regular part of ministry (Acts 5:16). And the Apostle Paul was also adept at dealing with demons (Acts 13:8-12, Acts 16:16-18).
- There are spiritual "rules of engagement" in the Scripture that give us tactics for dislodging demons. For most, these rules of engagement are learned through experience and talking with others who do this ministry. These biblical passages are normally overlooked unless you are engaged in spiritual warfare and setting people free from bondage.
- Ephesians 4:26-27 gives us the spiritual principle that sin, such as anger, gives the devil a "foothold." The Greek word for "foothold" means a "place to occupy." Unconfessed sin gives the enemy a right to occupy a place in our spiritual life. This forms a "spiritual oppression" over the person. The more unconfessed sin that exists in a person's life, the greater the strength of this spiritual oppression. Almost all Christian men struggling with pornography have an innate sense that the enemy is playing some role in their inability to stop the habit.
- We must discover what allowed the demon to gain this "place to occupy." Many people use the term of breaking the "legal rights" that the enemy must have to occupy a place.
- Based on 1 John 1:9, confessing sin is the first step in breaking this legal right of the enemy to oppress you.
- We use the authoritative term I *"bind every demon"* based on the principles found in Mark 3:27 and Matthew 12:29. We must bind the strongman. Binding demons is the first step of taking the authority given us in Christ to defeat the enemy. We start this binding process by praying *"In the name of Jesus."* We do not have power in our own authority, but like the disciples in Luke 10:17-20, we learn that demons only submit when confronted in Jesus' name. Paul gives us this pattern in Acts 16:18 when he says, "In the name of Jesus Christ I command you to come out of her!"
- If you are involved in ministry, at times demons may receive an "assignment to attack you" from the enemy through his people who "curse you" or by occultic members who are "praying against you." This is why we regularly pray for God to break curses and assignments in the Every Man A Pure Warrior Warfare Prayer.

- There is a hierarchy of sorts in the spiritual realm found in Ephesians 6:12. It talks of rulers, authorities, powers and spiritual forces of evil. Experience has taught us that higher-level demons will not let demons under their authority leave a person. This is why we say, *"I cut you off from your spiritual head"* in the Every Man A Pure Warrior Warfare Prayer.

- Once we have broken all the legal rights the enemy has, we must take our authority in Christ and tell him to leave. Demons don't just leave because they have lost their legal right to harass. We must command them to **"GO** *or be gone!"* We send them into the abyss, since Luke 8:31 reveals that demons are afraid and do not want to go there.

- We have someone say, *"I agree in the name of Jesus"* based on Matthew 18:18-19.

Most people who criticize the topic of spiritual warfare have never actually done any deliverance ministry. But *"setting captives free"* was a primary purpose for Jesus (Luke 4:18-19, 21). It seems that Matthew 28:20 would imply that we should do the same.

2 Corinthians 2:11 says, *"...in order that Satan might not outwit us. For we are not unaware of his schemes."* Most Christians have had almost no teaching on this subject, and many pastors admit that the subject was passed over in seminary. But as this verse teaches, we definitely *should* be keenly aware of the tactics of our enemy. Ignorance on our part only benefits the enemy, and many people have lived their whole lives under spiritual oppression when they could have lived in freedom.

Below is a partial list of authors that Bob Reehm and I have read in order to understand this issue more completely. Many of them share their journey of moving from a worldview that minimized the subject to a more Scriptural based and practical understanding of demonology.

Spiritual Warfare by Karl Payne

Destined to Overcome: The Technique of Spiritual Warfare by Paul Billheimer

The Adversary: The Christian Versus Demon Activity by Mark Bubeck

Overcoming the Adversary by Mark Bubeck

Defeating Dark Angels by Charles Kraft

I Give You Authority by Charles Kraft

The Bondage Breaker by Neil Anderson

The Beginner's Guide to Spiritual Warfare by Neil Anderson

THE EVERY MAN A WARRIOR ICON

The Every Man A Warrior icon is a symbol of a man's Quiet Time. God intended for you to be a warrior that worships the person of Jesus Christ. Your Quiet Time is a place of worship, but also a place to get ready for battle. Make it your objective to spend enough time with Jesus each day to do both: worship and prepare for war. Each is an important part of who you are as a man.

I Am a Warrior and I Kneel at the Cross

I kneel at the cross, battered and bruised, with blood on my wound and a shield that is used. My helmet is off, my face is scarred. I'm weary and tired. I'm a warrior and I kneel at the cross.

I am also a prince and a son of the King, with power and authority to rule. But instead, I give up my life to serve because I'm a warrior and I kneel at the cross.

I live as a light in a dark world of pain. I fight to set captives free from their prison and shame. I battle for truth and I count the cost. I'm a warrior and I kneel at the cross.

I reject the world with its brokenness and loss, because He died for me upon that cross. Now I have HOPE and a lasting reward. I'm a warrior and I kneel at the cross.

I'm coming home soon when my battles are won. To see my father's face and hear, "Well done my son. You are home at last, take your place at my side, because I chose you to be a warrior and you knelt at the cross."

—Lonnie Berger

EMAW QUIET TIME SHEETS

Additional EMAW Quiet Time sheets can be downloaded from the website:

www.everymanawarrior.com

EMOTIONAL PAIN WORDS[10]

Abandoned
Accused
Afraid
All my fault
Alone
Always wrong
Angry
Annihilated
Anxious
Apathetic
Ashamed
Avoided
Awkward
Babied
Bad
Belittled
Betrayed
Bewildered
Bitter
Blamed
Can't do anything right
Can't trust anyone
Cheap
Cheated
Coerced
Condemned
Confused
Conspired against
Controlled
Cornered
Crushed
Cursed
Cut off
Deceived
Defeated
Defenseless
Defrauded
Degraded
Depressed
Deprived
Deserted
Desires rejected
Despair
Despised
Despondent
Destroyed

Detested
Devalued
Didn't belong
Didn't measure up
Dirty
Disappointed
Discarded
Discounted
Discouraged
Disgraced
Dishonored
Disregarded
Disrespected
Dominated
Embarrassed
Empty
Excluded
Exhausted
Exploited
Exposed
Failure
Fear, fearful
Foolish
Forced
Forsaken
Friendless
Frightened
Frustrated
Good for nothing
Guilty
Hated
Hate myself
Helpless
Hopeless
Humiliated
Hurt
Hysterical
Ignored
Impure
Inadequate
Incompetent
Indecent
Inferior
Inhibited
Insecure
Insensitive to my needs

Insignificant
Invalidated
Isolated
Knocked down
Judged
Left out
Lied to
Lonely
Lost
Made fun of
Manipulated
Mistreated
Misunderstood
Mocked
Molested
Neglected
No good
No support
No way out
Not being affirmed
Not cared for
Not cherished
Not deserving to live
Not listened to
Not measure up
Not valued
Opinions not valued
Overwhelmed
Paralyzed
Powerless
Pressured
Pressure to perform
Publicly shamed
Put down
Rejected
Repulsed
Resentful
Revenge
Ridiculed
Ruined
Sad
Scared
Secluded
Self disgust
Separated
Shamed

Silenced
Stepped on
Shattered
Stressed
Stupid
Suicidal
Taken advantage of
Terrified
Threatened
Torn apart
Trapped
Trashed
Tricked
Ugly
Unable to speak
Unaccepted
Uncaring
Uncared for
Unchosen
Unclean
Undesireable
Unfairly judged
Unfairly treated
Unfit
Unimportant
Unheard
Unloved
Unlovable
Unnecessary
Unneeded
Unnoticed
Unprotected
Unresponsive
Unsafe
Unwanted
Useless
Valueless
Violated
Vulnerable
Walked on
Wasted
Weak
Worthless
Wounded

[10] © 2007 John Regier. Used by permission. John Regier, Caring for the Emotionally Damaged Heart, copyright 2009, page 8, self-published by Caring for the Heart Ministries, 3545 American Drive, Colorado Springs CO 80917

Quiet Time Journal

Date _____ Passage I Read Today _____

Major themes from all I read:

Best verse and thought for the day.
(Write the verse & your thoughts.)

Ask Questions

Is there:

A command to obey

A promise to claim

A sin to avoid

An application to make

Something new about God

Ask: Who, What, When, Where, Why

Emphasize:
Different words

Rewrite
In your own words

Communicate with God
W - Worship Him
A - Admit Sin
R - My Requests

Date _____ Passage I Read Today _____

Major themes from all I read:

Best verse and thought for the day.
(Write the verse & your thoughts.)

Ask Questions

Is there:

A command to obey

A promise to claim

A sin to avoid

An application to make

Something new about God

Ask: Who, What, When, Where, Why

Emphasize:
Different words

Rewrite
In your own words

Communicate with God
W - Worship Him
A - Admit Sin
R - My Requests

Quiet Time Journal

Date_____   Passage I Read Today_____

Major themes from all I read:

Best verse and thought for the day.
(Write the verse & your thoughts.)

Ask Questions

Is there:

A command to obey

A promise to claim

A sin to avoid

An application to make

Something new about God

Ask: Who, What, When, Where, Why

Emphasize:
Different words

Rewrite
In your own words

Communicate with God
W - Worship Him
A - Admit Sin
R - My Requests

Date_____   Passage I Read Today_____

Major themes from all I read:

Best verse and thought for the day.
(Write the verse & your thoughts.)

Ask Questions

Is there:

A command to obey

A promise to claim

A sin to avoid

An application to make

Something new about God

Ask: Who, What, When, Where, Why

Emphasize:
Different words

Rewrite
In your own words

Communicate with God
W - Worship Him
A - Admit Sin
R - My Requests

Quiet Time Journal

Date _____ Passage I Read Today _____

Major themes from all I read:

Best verse and thought for the day.
(Write the verse & your thoughts.)

Ask Questions

Is there:

A command to obey

A promise to claim

A sin to avoid

An application to make

Something new about God

Ask: Who, What, When, Where, Why

Emphasize:
Different words

Rewrite
In your own words

Communicate with God
W - Worship Him
A - Admit Sin
R - My Requests

Date _____ Passage I Read Today _____

Major themes from all I read:

Best verse and thought for the day.
(Write the verse & your thoughts.)

Ask Questions

Is there:

A command to obey

A promise to claim

A sin to avoid

An application to make

Something new about God

Ask: Who, What, When, Where, Why

Emphasize:
Different words

Rewrite
In your own words

Communicate with God
W - Worship Him
A - Admit Sin
R - My Requests

Quiet Time Journal

Date _____ Passage I Read Today _____

Major themes from all I read:

Ask Questions

Is there:

A command to obey

A promise to claim

A sin to avoid

An application to make

Something new about God

Ask: Who, What, When, Where, Why

Emphasize: Different words

Rewrite In your own words

Best verse and thought for the day.
(Write the verse & your thoughts.)

Communicate with God
W - Worship Him
A - Admit Sin
R - My Requests

Date _____ Passage I Read Today _____

Major themes from all I read:

Ask Questions

Is there:

A command to obey

A promise to claim

A sin to avoid

An application to make

Something new about God

Ask: Who, What, When, Where, Why

Emphasize: Different words

Rewrite In your own words

Best verse and thought for the day.
(Write the verse & your thoughts.)

Communicate with God
W - Worship Him
A - Admit Sin
R - My Requests

Quiet Time Journal

Date _____ Passage I Read Today _____

Major themes from all I read:

Best verse and thought for the day.
(Write the verse & your thoughts.)

Ask Questions

Is there:

A command to obey

A promise to claim

A sin to avoid

An application to make

Something new about God

Ask: Who, What, When, Where, Why

Emphasize:
Different words

Rewrite
In your own words

Communicate with God

W - Worship Him

A - Admit Sin

R - My Requests

Date _____ Passage I Read Today _____

Major themes from all I read:

Best verse and thought for the day.
(Write the verse & your thoughts.)

Ask Questions

Is there:

A command to obey

A promise to claim

A sin to avoid

An application to make

Something new about God

Ask: Who, What, When, Where, Why

Emphasize:
Different words

Rewrite
In your own words

Communicate with God

W - Worship Him

A - Admit Sin

R - My Requests

Quiet Time Journal

Date _____ Passage I Read Today _____

Major themes from all I read:

Best verse and thought for the day.
(Write the verse & your thoughts.)

Ask Questions

Is there:

A command to obey

A promise to claim

A sin to avoid

An application to make

Something new about God

Ask: Who, What, When, Where, Why

Emphasize:
Different words

Rewrite
In your own words

Communicate with God

W - Worship Him

A - Admit Sin

R - My Requests

Date _____ Passage I Read Today _____

Major themes from all I read:

Best verse and thought for the day.
(Write the verse & your thoughts.)

Ask Questions

Is there:

A command to obey

A promise to claim

A sin to avoid

An application to make

Something new about God

Ask: Who, What, When, Where, Why

Emphasize:
Different words

Rewrite
In your own words

Communicate with God

W - Worship Him

A - Admit Sin

R - My Requests

Quiet Time Journal

Date _____ Passage I Read Today _____

Major themes from all I read:

Best verse and thought for the day.
(Write the verse & your thoughts.)

Ask Questions

Is there:

A command to obey

A promise to claim

A sin to avoid

An application to make

Something new about God

Ask: Who, What, When, Where, Why

Emphasize:
Different words

Rewrite
In your own words

Communicate with God
W - Worship Him
A - Admit Sin
R - My Requests

Date _____ Passage I Read Today _____

Major themes from all I read:

Best verse and thought for the day.
(Write the verse & your thoughts.)

Ask Questions

Is there:

A command to obey

A promise to claim

A sin to avoid

An application to make

Something new about God

Ask: Who, What, When, Where, Why

Emphasize:
Different words

Rewrite
In your own words

Communicate with God
W - Worship Him
A - Admit Sin
R - My Requests

Quiet Time Journal

Date _____ Passage I Read Today _____

Major themes from all I read:

Best verse and thought for the day.
(Write the verse & your thoughts.)

Ask Questions

Is there:

A command to obey

A promise to claim

A sin to avoid

An application to make

Something new about God

Ask: Who, What, When, Where, Why

Emphasize:
Different words

Rewrite
In your own words

Communicate with God
W- Worship Him
A - Admit Sin
R - My Requests

Date _____ Passage I Read Today _____

Major themes from all I read:

Best verse and thought for the day.
(Write the verse & your thoughts.)

Ask Questions

Is there:

A command to obey

A promise to claim

A sin to avoid

An application to make

Something new about God

Ask: Who, What, When, Where, Why

Emphasize:
Different words

Rewrite
In your own words

Communicate with God
W- Worship Him
A - Admit Sin
R - My Requests

Quiet Time Journal

Date _____ Passage I Read Today _____

Major themes from all I read:

Best verse and thought for the day.
(Write the verse & your thoughts.)

Ask Questions

Is there:

A command to obey

A promise to claim

A sin to avoid

An application to make

Something new about God

Ask: Who, What, When, Where, Why

Emphasize:
Different words

Rewrite
In your own words

Communicate with God
W - Worship Him
A - Admit Sin
R - My Requests

Date _____ Passage I Read Today _____

Major themes from all I read:

Best verse and thought for the day.
(Write the verse & your thoughts.)

Ask Questions

Is there:

A command to obey

A promise to claim

A sin to avoid

An application to make

Something new about God

Ask: Who, What, When, Where, Why

Emphasize:
Different words

Rewrite
In your own words

Communicate with God
W - Worship Him
A - Admit Sin
R - My Requests

Quiet Time Journal

Date_____ Passage I Read Today_____

Major themes from all I read:

Best verse and thought for the day.
(Write the verse & your thoughts.)

Ask Questions

Is there:

A command to obey

A promise to claim

A sin to avoid

An application to make

Something new about God

Ask: Who, What, When, Where, Why

Emphasize:
Different words

Rewrite
In your own words

Communicate with God
W- Worship Him
A - Admit Sin
R - My Requests

Date_____ Passage I Read Today_____

Major themes from all I read:

Best verse and thought for the day.
(Write the verse & your thoughts.)

Ask Questions

Is there:

A command to obey

A promise to claim

A sin to avoid

An application to make

Something new about God

Ask: Who, What, When, Where, Why

Emphasize:
Different words

Rewrite
In your own words

Communicate with God
W- Worship Him
A - Admit Sin
R - My Requests

Completion Record
Course Requirements for Book 4

This course is designed for men who want to become the man God wants them to be. Change will only happen when you do the work and give it your best effort. The completion record is a tool designed to help you gauge your progress and help you encourage each other to succeed.

Have another member of your group check you on the requirements of this course. Have them initial and date each item.

Scripture Memory Record

I have memorized and quoted word-perfect:

INITIAL AND DATE

- WWW A MAP _____
- 1 Corinthians 10:13 _____
- Ephesians 5:3 _____
- Ecclesiastes 4:9-10 _____
- Romans 12:2 _____
- Psalm 119:9-11 _____
- Psalm 103:8-12 _____
- "Amazing Grace" _____
- Ephesians 6:11 _____
- Romans 6:13 _____
- Matthew 6:9-13 _____
- 1 Peter 5:8 _____
- Luke 4:13 _____
- 2 Corinthians 10:3-5 _____
- James 4:7 _____
- Ephesians 4:26-27 _____
- 2 Corinthians 2:11 _____

Psalm 62:8 _____

Psalm 86:11 _____

Isaiah 53:4-5 _____

1 Corinthians 6:18-20 _____

Galatians 2:20 _____

2 Corinthians 11:3 _____

Hebrews 13:4 _____

2 Peter 1:3-4 _____

Lesson Record

I have completed the following lessons in *Book 4; Every Man A Pure Warrior*.

INITIAL AND DATE

LESSON 1
Unlocking the Prison Doors of Pornography _____

LESSON 2
Battle Strategy Checklist _____

LESSON 3
Allies: Battle Buddies _____

LESSON 4
Scripture Memory: Key to Transformation _____

LESSON 5
Aggressive Worship Skill 1: Memorize Psalm 103:8-12 _____

LESSON 6
Aggressive Worship Skill 2: Singing Psalms, Hymns, and Spiritual Songs _____

LESSON 7
Aggressive Worship Skill 3: Daily Offering and Armoring Our Bodies for Warfare _____

LESSON 8
Spiritual Warfare 1: Was I Under Demonic Attack? _____

LESSON 9
Spiritual Warfare 2: The Jesus Warfare Model _____

LESSON 10
Spiritual Warfare 3: Steps to Resist Demonic Oppression _____

LESSON 11
　Wounds 1: "Porn is Meeting a Need in Your Life

LESSON 12
　Wounds 2: Connecting Your Heart to God

LESSON 13
　Wounds 3: Forgiveness: Removing the Thorn of Woundedness

LESSON 14
　Amputation and Blockade

LESSON 15
　Preach the Gospel to Yourself Daily

LESSON 16
　Radical Transformation

LESSON 17
　Hope: Review and Apply

WWW A MAP PRACTICE RECORD

INITIAL AND DATE

From Lessons 7, 11 and 17; pages 80, 130 & 201, add up how many times you practiced WWW A MAP.

COURSE REQUIREMENTS FOR COMPLETION OF BOOK 4

INITIAL AND DATE

- Finished all seventeen lessons.

- Memorized and quoted all Scripture passages.

- Since EMAW and *Every Man A Pure Warrior* have impacted my life, I have prayerfully considered supporting the ministry of EMAW on a monthly basis. If God leads you to give, please go to: everymanawarrior.com and click on donate. All donations are tax-deductible and help advance the ministry of EMAW around the world.

Congratulations! You have finished Book 4 of this course.

Purity Pack NIV Verses

Allies James 5:16

Allies Hebrews 10:24-25

Attitude Romans 13:13-14

Attitude Colossians 3:5-7

The Body Romans 6:12-13

The Body 1 Corinthians 6:18-20

Buddy Needed Ecclesiastes 4:9-10

Buddy Needed Hebrews 3:13

Buddy Needed Proverbs 27:17

Conscience Acts 24:16

Conscience 1 Timothy 1:5

Consequences 1 Corinthians 6:9-10

Consequences Proverbs 5:7-10

Consequences Proverbs 5:11-14

Consequences Hebrews 13:4

Destiny Ephesians 1:4-5

Destiny Colossians 1:21-22

Destiny Matthew 5:8

Discipline Proverbs 5:21-23

Discipline 2 Corinthians 7:1

Discipline 2 Timothy 2:20-21

Eyes Matthew 5:28

Eyes Matthew 6:22-23

Eyes Job 31:1

Eyes Psalm 101:3

Flee Genesis 39:12

Flee 2 Timothy 2:22

Forgiveness 1 John 1:9

Forgiveness Psalm 51:1-4

Forgiveness Psalm 51:5-9

Forgiveness Psalm 130:3-4

God Psalm 62:8

God Lamentations 3:22-23

God Isaiah 6:3

God 1 Peter 1:15-16

God Psalm 130:3-4

Grace Titus 2:11-12

Grace Hebrews 4:16

Grace Philippians 2:12-13

Grace 1 Corinthians 15:10

Habits Ephesians 4:22-24

Habits Romans 6:17-18

Heart Psalm 119:9-11

Heart Matthew 15:18-19

Holy Spirit Galatians 5:22-23

Holy Spirit Ephesians 5:18

Holy Spirit John 14:26

Holy Spirit Romans 8:11-14

Holy Spirit Zechariah 4:6

Homosexuality Romans 1:25-27

Homosexuality Leviticus 18:22

Hope Psalm 3:5

Hope Philippians 1:6

Jesus 1 John 3:2-3

Jesus Hebrews 2:18

Jesus 1 John 1:7

Marriage Proverbs 5:15-19

Marriage 1 Corinthians 7:2-5

Masturbation Psalm 19:14

Masturbation 1 Corinthians 6:12

Masturbation Luke 9:23

Masturbation Titus 2:6

Prostitutes 1 Corinthians 6:15-16

Prostitutes Proverbs 23:27-28

Prostitutes Proverbs 6:23-26

Reckon Romans 6:11

Reckon Galatians 2:20

Resist James 4:7-8

Resist Matthew 4:10-11

Restoration Psalm 51:10-12

Restoration Luke 22:31-32

Restoration 1 Corinthians 6:11

Satan 1 Peter 5:8-9

Satan Luke 4:13

Satan John 10:10

Secret Sins Psalm 90:7-8

Secret Sins Numbers 32:23

Secret Sins Matthew 10:26

Standards 1 John 2:15-17

Standards Isaiah 32:8

Standards Ephesians 5:3

Temptation 1 Corinthians 10:13

Temptation James 1:13-16

Thoughts Romans 8:5-7

Thoughts Philippians 4:8

Thoughts Colossians 3:1-2

Thoughts 2 Corinthians 10:5

Spiritual War Revelation 12:17

Spiritual War 1 Peter 2:11

Weapons Ephesians 6:17

Weapons Jeremiah 23:29

Weapons 2 Peter 1:3-4

Weapons 2 Corinthians 10:3-4

Weapons Hebrews 4:12

MAKING A DIFFERENCE FOR ONLY $1 PER DAY

Men,

Would you give up a cup of coffee to help another man get started in Every Man A Warrior? A cup of coffee costs about $1. A gift of $1 per day, $30 per month will help us put all four EMAW books and verse pack into the hands of another man somewhere in the world. Your small sacrifice could help one man each month or 12 men per year. Each man you touch with this gift, normally has a wife and several children whose lives are also transformed.

Men, if Every Man A Warrior has changed your life, then help another man each month have that same life-changing experience.

When these men multiply, leading groups of their own, your life can touch hundreds, all because you gave away a cup of coffee, $1 a day. ***Would you give this $1 per day decision your most serious consideration?***

Go to **www.EveryManAWarrior.com** to donate. Click the "Donate to EMAW" button. Click on $30 per month and check the "Make this a monthly payment?" box.

Make your life count for the eternal with only one cup of coffee each day. And while you are drinking your favorite brew, pray for these men. Your life and prayers can change the world.

Thank you,
Lonnie Berger

ABOUT THE AUTHOR: BOB REEHM

Since 1982, Bob Reehm has been on staff with The Navigators, an international Christian organization known for its expertise in discipleship and leadership development.

Bob and his wife Char currently live in Marina, California and they both minister at two military bases in Monterey: The Naval Post Graduate School and the Defense Language Institute. They have three adult children and seven grandchildren.

Bob was first introduced to the world of pornography when he was ten years old after his parents divorced. Immediately thereafter, he found comfort through enslavement to sexual sin. Seven years later, when a senior in High School, he met Christ at an evangelistic music crusade. Soon after that, he met The Navigators during his freshman year at the US Naval Academy. It took him four years of discipleship training before figuring out that 1 Corinthians 10:13 was true, that sexual sin was common to man and his battle for purity began in earnest.

After graduation, with a degree in Chemistry, and another year of post-graduate training in Nuclear Engineering, Bob served in the Reactor Department of the USS Enterprise, then as the Damage Control Assistant on the USS Bainbridge. He married his wife Char in 1980, and then served two more years in the Navy before God called both him and his wife into full-time vocational ministry with The Navigators.

They pioneered a ministry at the Naval Amphibious Base in Coronado, California, then ministered for six years at Naval Air Station Alameda, California. In 1989, they moved to Marina and have ministered to the military on the Monterey Peninsula for the last thirty years.

In 1997, Bob's first book, The War Within: Gaining Victory in the Battle for Sexual Purity was published under the pen name Robert Daniels. It was endorsed by Promise Keepers and won Amazon.com Best Seller in the category of Christian Counseling. He has been speaking and writing on sexual purity for the last 30 years both in the United States and around the world.

In 2012, Bob met Lonnie Berger, who invited him to write this Book 4 of the EMAW series, Every Man A Pure Warrior. It's been field-tested with over 300 men so far and has undergone five rewrites. One of Bob's life verses is Luke 22:31-32 (TLB) "Simon, Simon, Satan has desired to have you, to sift you like wheat, but I have pleaded in prayer for you that your faith should not completely fail. So when you have repented and turned to me again, strengthen and build up the faith of your brothers." Every Man A Pure Warrior is a fulfillment of this command to strengthen and build up the faith of my brothers in Christ.

Every Man A Warrior materials are sold exclusively at www.everymanawarrior.com and www.emapw.com. Use this website to download video and audio resources, or find upcoming Every Man A Warrior conferences in your area.

EVERY MAN A WARRIOR - Book 4

Ephesians 5:3

But among you there must not be even a hint of sexual immorality, or of any kind of impurity, or of greed, because these are improper for God's holy people.

Ephesians 5:3

LESSON 2
Battle Strategy Checklist

EVERY MAN A WARRIOR - Book 4

Psalm 103:8-12

The Lord is compassionate and gracious, slow to anger, abounding in love. He will not always accuse, nor will he harbor his anger forever; he does not treat us as our sins deserve or repay us according to our iniquities. For as high as the heavens are above the earth, so great is his love for those who fear him; as far as the east is from the west, so far has he removed our transgressions from us.

Psalm 103:8-12

LESSON 5
Aggressive Worship Skill 1: Memorize Psalms 103:8-12

EVERY MAN A WARRIOR - Book 4

WWW A MAP — 7 Principles for Sexual Purity

Worship
Warfare Praying
Wounds and Triggers
Amputate
Memorize Scripture
Allies
Preach the Gospel to Yourself Daily

LESSON 1
Unlocking the Prison Doors

EVERY MAN A WARRIOR - Book 4

Romans 12:2

Do not conform to the pattern of this world, but be transformed by the renewing of your mind. Then you will be able to test and approve what God's will is—his good, pleasing and perfect will.

Romans 12:2

LESSON 4
Scripture Memory: Key to Transformation

LESSON 3
Allies: Battle Buddies

ECCLESIASTES 4:9-10

Two are better than one, because they have a good return for their labor: If either of them falls down, one can help the other up. But pity anyone who falls and has no one to help them up.

ECCLESIASTES 4:9-10

AMAZING GRACE!

Amazing Grace! How sweet the sound
That saved a wretch like me.
I once was lost, but now am found,
Was blind, but now I see.

'Twas grace that taught my heart to fear,
And grace my fears relieved.
How precious did that grace appear,
The hour I first believed.

Through many dangers, toils and snares
I have already come;
'Tis grace has brought me safe thus far
And grace will lead me home.

When we've been there ten thousand years
Bright shining as the sun,
We've no less days to sing God's praise
Than when we've first begun.

LESSON 6
Aggressive Worship Skill 2: Singing Psalms, Hymns, and Spiritual Songs

LESSON 1
Unlocking the Prison Doors

1 CORINTHIANS 10:13

No temptation has overtaken you except what is common to mankind. And God is faithful; he will not let you be tempted beyond what you can bear. But when you are tempted, he will also provide a way out so that you can endure it.

1 CORINTHIANS 10:13

PSALM 119:9-11

How can a young person stay on the path of purity?
By living according to your word. I seek you with all my heart; do not let me stray from your commands.
I have hidden your word in my heart that I might not sin against you.

PSALM 119:9-11

LESSON 4
Scripture Memory: Key to Transformation

EVERY MAN A WARRIOR - Book 4

The Lord's Prayer

MATTHEW 6:9-13

Our Father in heaven, hallowed be your name, your kingdom come, your will be done, on earth as it is in heaven. Give us today our daily bread. And forgive us our debts, as we also have forgiven our debtors. And lead us not into temptation, but deliver us from the evil one, for yours is the kingdom and the power and the glory forever. Amen.

MATTHEW 6:9-13

LESSON 8
Spiritual Warfare 1: Was I Under Demonic Attack?

EVERY MAN A WARRIOR - Book 4

JAMES 4:7

Submit yourselves, then, to God. Resist the devil, and he will flee from you.

JAMES 4:7

LESSON 10
Advanced Spiritual Warfare: Steps to Resist Demonic Oppression

---

EVERY MAN A WARRIOR - Book 4

EPHESIANS 6:11

Put on the full armor of God, so that you can take your stand against the devil's schemes.

EPHESIANS 6:11

LESSON 7
Worship to Warfare Skill 3:
Daily Offering and Armoring Our Bodies for Warfare

EVERY MAN A WARRIOR - Book 4

LUKE 4:13

When the devil had finished all this tempting, he left him until an opportune time.

LUKE 4:13

LESSON 9
Spiritual Warfare: The Jesus Model

EVERY MAN A WARRIOR - Book 4

LESSON 8
Spiritual Warfare 1: Was I Under Demonic Attack?

1 PETER 5:8

Be alert and of sober mind. Your enemy the devil prowls around like a roaring lion looking for someone to devour.

1 PETER 5:8

EVERY MAN A WARRIOR - Book 4

LESSON 10
Advanced Spiritual Warfare: Steps to Resist Demonic Oppression

EPHESIANS 4:26-27

In your anger do not sin: Do not let the sun go down while you are still angry, and do not give the devil a foothold.

EPHESIANS 4:26-27

EVERY MAN A WARRIOR - Book 4

LESSON 7
Worship to Warfare Skill 3:
Daily Offering and Armoring Our Bodies for Warfare

ROMANS 6:13

Do not offer any part of yourself to sin as an instrument of wickedness, but rather offer yourselves to God as those who have been brought from death to life; and offer every part of yourself to him as an instrument of righteousness.

ROMANS 6:13

EVERY MAN A WARRIOR - Book 4

LESSON 9
Spiritual Warfare: The Jesus Model

2 CORINTHIANS 10:3-5

For though we live in the world, we do not wage war as the world does. The weapons we fight with are not the weapons of the world. On the contrary, they have divine power to demolish strongholds. We demolish arguments and every pretension that sets itself up against the knowledge of God, and we take captive every thought to make it obedient to Christ.

2 CORINTHIANS 10:3-5

EVERY MAN A WARRIOR - Book 4

PSALM 86:11

Teach me your way, Lord, that I may rely on your faithfulness; give me an undivided heart, that I may fear your name.

PSALM 86:11

LESSON 12
Wounds 2: Connecting Your Heart to God

EVERY MAN A WARRIOR - Book 4

GALATIANS 2:20

I have been crucified with Christ and I no longer live, but Christ lives in me. The life I now live in the body, I live by faith in the Son of God, who loved me and gave himself for me.

GALATIANS 2:20

LESSON 15
Preach the Gospel to Yourself Daily

EVERY MAN A WARRIOR - Book 4

2 CORINTHIANS 2:11

... in order that Satan might not outwit us. For we are not unaware of his schemes.

2 CORINTHIANS 2:11

LESSON 10
Advanced Spiritual Warfare: Steps to Resist Demonic Oppression

---

EVERY MAN A WARRIOR - Book 4

1 CORINTHIANS 6:18-20

Flee from sexual immorality. All other sins a person commits are outside the body, but whoever sins sexually, sins against their own body. Do you not know that your bodies are temples of the Holy Spirit, who is in you, whom you have received from God? You are not your own; you were bought at a price. Therefore honor God with your bodies.

1 CORINTHIANS 6:18-20

LESSON 14
Radical Amputation

LESSON 13
Wounds 3: Forgiveness: Removing the Thorn of Woundedness

ISAIAH 53:4-5

Surely he took up our pain and bore our suffering, yet we considered him punished by God, stricken by him, and afflicted. But he was pierced for our transgressions, he was crushed for our iniquities; the punishment that brought us peace was on him, and by his wounds we are healed.

ISAIAH 53:4-5

LESSON 15
Preach the Gospel to Yourself Daily

2 CORINTHIANS 11:3

But I am afraid that just as Eve was deceived by the serpent's cunning, your minds may somehow be led astray from your sincere and pure devotion to Christ.

2 CORINTHIANS 11:3

LESSON 11
Wounds 1: "Porn is Meeting a Need in Your Life"

PSALM 62:8

Trust in him at all times, you people; pour out your hearts to him, for God is our refuge.

PSALM 62:8

EVERY MAN A WARRIOR - Book 4

2 PETER 1:3-4

His divine power has given us everything we need for a godly life through our knowledge of him who called us by his own glory and goodness. Through these he has given us his very great and precious promises, so that through them you may participate in the divine nature, having escaped the corruption in the world caused by evil desires.

2 PETER 1:3-4

LESSON 17
HOPE: Review and Apply

EVERY MAN A WARRIOR - Book 4

HEBREWS 13:4

Marriage should be honored by all, and the marriage bed kept pure, for God will judge the adulterer and all the sexually immoral.

HEBREWS 13:4

LESSON 16
Radical Transformation

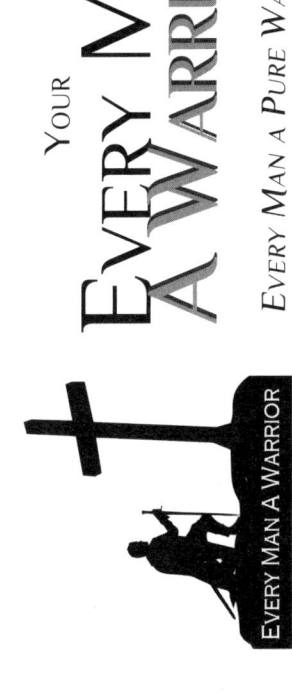

YOUR

Every Man A Warrior

EVERY MAN A PURE WARRIOR
VERSE PACK

This pack belongs to: _____

Phone: _____

Worship

- Start worshiping God by praising Him. Sing your favorite hymn, psalm, or worship song. Offer your body and body parts to God as an act of worship and clothe your body with the armor of God.

Warfare Praying

- First, confess any known sin by praying and say the following spiritual warfare prayer. "Lord Jesus, I ask forgiveness for _____ [name any sin that comes to mind such as looking at porn, masturbation, lust, anger, unforgiveness, greed, or hate]."

- Pray the Lord's Prayer: "Our Father in heaven, hallowed be your name, your kingdom come, your will be done, on earth as it is in heaven. Give us today our daily bread, and forgive us our debts, as we also have forgiven our debtors. And lead us not into temptation, but deliver us from the evil one, for yours is the kingdom and the power and the glory forever. Amen" (Matthew 6:9-13).

- After praying the prayer, personalize it for your temptation. "Lord, please deliver me from the Tempter who is tempting me to _____. Lord, please deliver me from the Accuser who is telling me that my sin is not forgiven." If you are praying with a partner, the partner should say, "I agree in the name of Jesus."

Wounds and Triggers

- Ask the Holy Spirit to show you any wounds that are causing you to act out. Extend forgiveness to anyone who has hurt you. "Lord, I extend forgiveness to_____ for _____."

Amputate

- Separate yourself from any source of porn or lust-inducing environments. If you have just seen a pretty woman who is triggering you, begin to pray for her salvation, that she would find Christ and walk with Him.

Memorize Scripture

- Review your Scripture verses. Begin quoting out loud the verses from Psalm 103, Romans 6, EMAW verses, or any other memorized passages of Scripture.

Allies

- Call a brother for prayer when tempted, confess if you have blown it, and begin to go through these seven principles together.

Preach the Gospel to Yourself Daily

- "I thank You, Father, for the truth that 'there is now no condemnation for those who are in Christ Jesus' (Romans 8:1). I thank You, Jesus, for dying on the cross for me. I praise You that I am forgiven. You look at me as if I had never sinned, and I am adopted into Your family. You purchased me, and now I am free from sin."

The WWW A MAP Model to Guide You in Being a Good Ally

1. **Discuss worship.** Ask your man, "How is your personal worship going?" Then spend some time worshiping together. Review portions of Psalm 103 or some other psalm that you've memorized and work through it verse by verse, praising and worshiping God.

    Work through the skills of worship. Offer your body and your body parts to God as an act of worship. Mention specifically in prayer each body part involved in sin.

    Review the words to your favorite song, hymn, psalm, or spiritual song. Worship God in the midst of the song.

    Worship God by putting on the armor of God, mentioning each piece by name. Follow this by putting on the new nature, love, and Jesus.

2. **Discuss warfare.** Pray together the Lord's Prayer focusing on the holiness of God (verse 9) and lead us not into temptation (verse 13). Name the temptation, for example, watching porn, lust, masturbation, or something else. And focus on, deliver us from the Evil One. Name how you are being attacked: by temptation, by accusation, by slander, or by other means, taking back the spiritual ground that was yielded to the Evil One.

3. **Move on to wounds.** What triggered you to sin? What wound was revealed through this sin? What inner needs were you seeking to meet? Come before God's throne, identifying the wound and asking God to both heal the wound and to help you forgive the person who caused the wound.

4. **Discuss the amputate step**. Ask about the delivery system for porn or whatever caused the sin. Ask: How are you going to disable or remove or eliminate the platform that is delivering sin to you?

5. **Next ask about their Scripture memory times and their review plans.** The battle for purity takes place in the mind. Review key Scriptures together.

6. **Close the WWW A MAP session by preaching and reviewing the gospel with each other.** Review the wonderful beauty of the sacrificial life, death and resurrection of Jesus. We are redeemed by the blood (Ephesians 1:7), are forgiven by the blood (Ephesians 1:7), are justified by the blood (Romans 5:9), are sanctified by the blood (Hebrews 13:12), and are being cleansed by the blood (1 John 1:7). Assure your friend that he is in fact forgiven (1 John 1:9, and James 5:16).

End in more worship, thanking God for the absolute cleansing and forgiveness of Jesus.

If you work through these steps, you are proving to be an ally in the struggle for holiness.

Remind your friend that he will be more vulnerable now that he has fallen. Satan will attack with guilt and shame and will attack God's promises by saying, "You are not forgiven." We must be on guard to resist these attacks after confession is made.